Decisions, Decisions, Decisions

Reading Tractate Horayot *of the Babylonian Talmud*

Joshua A. Fogel

Hamilton Books

A member of
The Rowman & Littlefield Publishing Group
Lanham • Boulder • New York • Toronto • Plymouth, UK

Copyright © 2013 by Hamilton Books
4501 Forbes Boulevard, Suite 200, Lanham, Maryland 20706
Hamilton Books Aquisitions Department (301) 459-3366

10 Thornbury Road, Plymouth PL6 7PP, United Kingdom

All rights reserved

British Library Cataloguing in Publication Information Available

Library of Congress Control Number: 2013936497
ISBN: 978-0-7618-6131-7 (paperback : alk. paper)—ISBN: 978-0-7618-6132-4 (electronic)

"A mamzer who is a Torah scholar
takes priority over a High Priest who is an idiot."
Horayot 13a

Contents

Author's Introduction	1
1 The Court Ruled (*dapim* 2a-6b)	3
2 The Anointed Priest Ruled (*dapim* 6b-9b)	43
3 An Anointed Priest Sinned (*dapim* 9b-14a)	61
Glossary of Selected Terms	97
Index of Tannaim and Amoraim	101
Index to Biblical and Rabbinic References	103

Author's Introduction

Decisions, decisions, decisions. What happens when you make a mistake? If the implications of the mistake affect only you, then any damage is at least limited in a human sense. But, if the implications affect a whole community, then the mistake can have a much greater and deleterious impact. That is the general theme of the tractate entitled *Horayot* (Decisions), in particular the erroneous rulings by authorities leading to the commission of sins by a wider public that may proceed to violate Torah prescriptions. Although this tractate is relatively short, each of its thirteen *dapim* (folio pages) is packed tightly with rulings and case studies, and the printed Talmudic pages are just as tightly packed with the commentaries of the great rabbis of yesteryear. The underlying question asked repeatedly is "What if?" If the court erroneously rules in such-and-such a manner, what do we do? If an individual acts in such-and-such a manner, what is to be done? What role does intentionality play? Where does responsibility lie, and how are sanctions meted out, when necessary? There being many such instances possible, and (to be sure) many more rabbis with opinions, one can certainly expect lots of disputation to ensue.

Decisions, yes, but these are all, at this point in time, entirely hypothetical. As long as there is no Temple standing, none of the material in this modest tractate has any practical application. In fact, all of the brilliant, fantastic debates and logical reasoning contained herein would have to have transpired in post-Temple times, meaning it was all unconnected in a substantive way to actual practice. Did the rabbis believe that the erection of the Third Temple was imminent? Perhaps some did. More likely, many of them felt that all of the details of the many Temple services had to be worked out before God actually brought the Third Temple into existence. Actually, given the radical differences of opinion among the rabbis about the Temple complex itself, it would require divine intervention to clear up many areas of disagreement. In any event, historical interest in how the many Temple services were handled would certainly have been insufficient to arouse the passions exhibited over the course of the centuries to follow.

Welcome to the realm of theoretical *halachah*. Unlike the rulings in tractates of the Talmud concerned with marriage and divorce, holidays such as Rosh Hashanah and Yom Kippur and Sukkot, business dealings, and much more that exerted powerful influences on the daily lives of traditional Jews over the entire post-Temple era, theoretical *halachah* concerns matters in a Temple-centered, Jerusalem-centered universe of Judaism.

Chapter One

The Court Ruled
(*dapim* 2a-6b)

HORAYOT 2

If someone accidentally violates a negative commandment of the Torah that would have spelled excision (*karet*) in a case of purposeful violation, he is required to bring a sin offering (*chatat*) to the Temple. Accidental errors usually involve individual mistakes about a given situation (such as mistakenly believing an item of food kosher when it wasn't) or about the law itself (such as being ignorant of the Torah's prohibition on a certain item of food, such as a rare or unidentified fish). Our first Mishnah in this tractate, though, concerns a third type of error. After the court meets to consider a given act, it rules that act to be allowed; a person then acts in accordance with the court's decision. That's fine, but the court later learns that it ruled incorrectly out of ignorance or improper available information. What is the individual, who has sinned not as a result of his own inadvertent error or ignorance, but as a result of the court's misconceived ruling, to do? Hmm.

So, if the court issued such a mistaken ruling concerning a commandment which would be punishable by *karet* for deliberate commission, and someone acted on this ruling, he is not liable to bring a *chatat*—whether he performs the act together with the court, after the court does so, or on his own. The reason is that he relied on the court's ruling; this was not a personal mistake, one made on one's own initiative.

Now for a complication. Let us say that the court issued such a mistaken decision. Then, one of its judges realized the errors of its ways, or one of the judges' disciples who, by virtue of his high level of learning, was fit to offer an opinion realized the error. Despite such a realization, this judge or disciple nonetheless acted in accordance with the mistaken ruling because of a misconception that they should follow the sages even if you know them to be in error. These fellows must bring a *chatat*, because they did not rely on the court. (I, for one, am going to need some help from the Gemara on this one.) The Mishnah concludes with a general rule that reliance on oneself in the commission of an inadvertent violation requires a *chatat*; reliance on the court does not lead to liability as such.

The Torah explicitly notes that if a ruling leads to a majority of the community transgressing a commandment, that community must bring a "communal-error bull" (*par helem davar shel tzibur*); the rabbis also teach that this level of error refers solely to the Great Sanhedrin of seventy-one judges. What is such a ruling by the court? The great sage Shmuel begins the Gemara's commentary by noting that, only when the court issues its ruling and explicitly says "you are allowed" to do X, does it reach liability for a "communal-error bull." Rav Dimi from Nehardea goes one step further: the court must explicitly say "you are allowed to do." In other words, in both cases but even more explicitly in Rav Dimi's rendition, it must be a ruling on an actual case brought before it.

Abaye agrees with Rav Dimi and cites another Mishnah (*Sanhedrin* 86b) dealing with the infamous "rebellious sage" (*zaken mamrei*), a scholar who rejects a ruling of the Sanhedrin and continues to rule contrariwise. If such a "sage" learns that the Sanhedrin overruled his position and he nonetheless continues teaching as he had before, he is not considered a "rebellious sage"; if he actually coaches people to act as per his now overruled position, he is liable as a "rebellious sage," punishment for which is the death penalty (gulp!). Abaye's point appears to be that such a rabbi is not liable until he actually instructs people to do X after learning that the court has ruled against him.

R. Abba adds more in support of Rav Dimi with a Mishnah (*Yevamot* 87b) concerning a woman waiting for testimony from a second witness that her husband has died—that being the law before she is allowed to remarry. If the court goes ahead and allows her to remarry, and she begins a sexual liaison prior to going through the first stage of the marriage process (betrothal or *kiddushin*) before which consummation is not allowed, and then (on top of all that) her long-lost husband turns up, she is legally responsible for a *chatat*. The court allowed her to remarry, not to carry on an affair. Ravina piles on another line of support for Rav Dimi, and the case is closed.

The Gemara now recapitulates the entire case with the views of Shmuel and Rav Dimi reversed. No surprise—the same ultimate conclusion but with Shmuel's position confirmed. If we only had the views of Shmuel and Rav Dimi, such a switch wouldn't be such a giant error, but with the three Mishnayot offered by Abaye, R. Abba, and Ravina, we have to conceive of their raising these instances not as support for Rav Dimi but now as efforts to dispute his opposition to Shmuel.

The actual text of our Mishnah states that "an individual...acted inadvertently, on their word." The Gemara now asks why we need both "on their word" and "inadvertently," inasmuch as they appear to be redundant. Rava helps us here. The term "inadvertently" (*shogeg*) refers to the court allowing the consumption of some sort of prohibited fat, which an individual mixed up with another piece of kosher fat he planned to eat, and then went and ate the prohibited fat. In such an instance, no *chatat* is required. The expression "on their word" refers to a case in which an individual followed the court's ruling and ate the piece of fat ruled allowed—no *chatat* required. Thus, Rava reads the Mishnah's passage as referring to two separate cases.

Another rendition is offered now of Rava's reading that makes it a single case—to be understood as a person who relied on the court's ruling and ate a piece of prohibited fat. In this rendition, the two expressions are understood to be reinforcing one another. Acting on the court's ruling requires no *chatat*; if he wanted the kosher piece of fat and "inadvertently" ate the prohibited piece, he is responsible for a *chatat*.

Rami bar Chama heard this explanation by Rava and had his doubts. So he asked about the law in such a case. Rava explained it to him as in our first rendering of his views: two different cases. Rami bar Chama doesn't buy it and suggests a ruling along the lines of the second rendering of Rava's views. So, the Gemara recaps Rava's second rendering, only to repudiate it in favor of the first. This is getting very confusing.

As it turns out, other rabbis of antiquity also were curious about Rami bar Chama's view. In our case—the court rules some piece of prohibited fat allowed and a person confuses it with a piece of kosher fat—Rav rules him not responsible for a *chatat*, while R. Yochanan rules him liable. The view of R. Yochanan is now rebutted with a slew of biblical verses about behavioral inadvertence. The pattern of a person's behavior is critical here, as R. Shimon ben Yose points out. The person whom R. Yochanan would charge with a *chatat* for inadvertent consumption of prohibited fat would ordinarily not stop his violation were he informed of the error. He thinks it's allowed by the court, and he's just the sort who will eat it as a result. Not so simple. Rav Pappa inserts here that R. Yochanan would argue that the court would reverse its ruling as soon as it was made aware of the error and that such a transgressor as we have concocted here would indeed cease eating such fats. In this case, he stops violating the law as soon as he learns the correct behavior, thus making him responsible for a *chatat*.

The Mishnah offered three scenarios for violating a court-sanctioned transgression which does not result in *chatat*: the court and the individual acted together, the court went first and the individual followed suit, and the court did not act and the individual did. So, what's up with this? Why did the Mishnah need to explicitly mention all three cases? These are not questions meant to overturn a Mishnah, but rather looking for an explanation, the assumption being that there has to be a reason which at present is still not clear.

[a→b]

In this case, the Gemara contends that the style of the Mishnah is meant to imply that the first of the three is its ruling and the others are "needless to say" so. Thus, "this and needless to say this" (*zo veeyn tzarich lomar zo*) is the formula, which appears only rarely in the Talmud.

The Mishnah next ruled that, if a member of the court or a disciple recognized that an error had been made and nonetheless acted in accordance with the (erroneous) ruling, they are liable for a *chatat*. The question raised asks a similar question to the one above: Why are both of these instances involved? Rava explains that, without inclusion of both, one might assume the ruling applied only to someone who knows the law and is able to render judgments on its basis (that is, a judge), whereas a disciple knows much about the law but is not yet able to offer a legal judgment. The Mishnah thus is meant to dismiss this idea—both a judge and a disciple are included.

Abaye responds to Rava that a close reading of the Mishnah reveals that the reference is to a "disciple who was worthy of offering rulings." That would seem to imply someone both learned in the law and able to offer judgments. Rava effectively responds that he meant to include such a distinction in his explanation. If the

Mishnah had not been explicit, one might think it covers a disciple both learned in the law and able to reach legal judgments, but a disciple without the latter quality would be exempt from a *chatat*. Thus, to dismiss such an error, the Mishnah added "worthy of offering rulings" to cover both a disciple learned but not able, as well as one not learned but able. This last odd ruling concerning a disciple "able to judge but not learned" in the law is deleted by a number of later authorities—for obvious reasons: it's quite odd.

The Gemara now asks for a bit more clarification: What constitutes a disciple "worthy of ruling?" Rava introduces the examples of Shimon ben Azzai and Shimon ben Zoma, both men capable of judging on the basis of their learning but never ordained as rabbis. Great scholars though they were, both died young and hence are referred to as "disciples." Abaye counters that the case we are dealing with involves someone who would not follow the court's decision if he knows it to be erroneous. If he did, he would be someone who deliberately transgressed the law, and a *chatat* is only offered for the inadvertent commission of sins. Rava rebuts with a *baraita* which explicitly mentions Shimon ben Azzai as a disciple worthy of offering rulings, and that he is responsible for the bringing a *chatat* for following the court's ruling—hence, he is not regarded as a deliberate violator of the law. The inadvertence lies in his erroneously following the principle of following the words of the sages a bit too assiduously.

The Mishnah ended with a general (summary) ruling (in the form of: *zeh haklal*, meaning that the general rule or law is X): If one relies on his own judgment and errs by violating a commandment, he must bring a *chatat*; if one relies on the court's judgment and transgresses the law, there is no liability. The Gemara wants some more specificity: The first half of the general ruling includes whom? Answer: Those who would defy a court ruling as a rule and prefer to come to their own conclusions with respect to the implementation of the law. How about the second half? It would include cases in which the court allowed something carrying a punishment of excision and then realized its error and withdrew the earlier ruling. If someone did not learn of the retraction and acted in accord with the court's erroneous decision, still no *chatat* is required.

The Gemara dismisses this out of hand, because it is stated explicitly in our next Mishnah—it is important to note that the Gemara always assumes no precedence by the order in which the Mishnayot, *baraitot*, and Gemaras are cited; they are always mutually interactive across the same tractate and indeed among all the other tractates (even those for which we now have no Gemara). The Gemara responds to its own rejection by arguing that a general law is taught before specifics are offered.

Back to the first part of our Mishnah and a discussion indicating a lack of unanimity on one of its assertions. I find this especially interesting, because there are relatively few such cases where the Mishnah is brought into question itself. Reporting the words of Shmuel, Rav Yehudah notes that the Mishnah echoes the view of R. Yehudah, but the sages argue that anyone who transgressed the law by following a court ruling is responsible for bringing a *chatat* to the Temple. What, asks the Gemara, is the basis of this contention that there was a dispute between R. Yehudah and the sages? A *baraita* notes the pertinent biblical phrase (*Leviticus* 4:27, emphasis added): "If a *soul* [a person]—from among the people of the land—should sin inadvertently by *his* transgressing *one* of the commandments of God that are not to be done." (In his translation of the Bible, *The Five Books of Moses: A Translation with Commentary* [New York and London: W. W. Norton & Company, 2004], Robert Alter [hereafter, Alter] renders this: "And if a single person from the common people should offend errantly in doing one of the LORD's commands that should not be done.") The *baraita* reads this as having three "exclusionary terms" (note the italicized terms above), all superfluous and hence purposefully inserted and hence fecund with implications. In this construction, "by *his* transgressing" is assumed to mean that the person involved acted on *his* own and is thus liable to a *chatat*; reliance on the court in committing an error results in no liability. Rav Yehudah attributes this *baraita* (on the surface quite anonymous) to R. Yehudah.

Rav Yehudah locates the view of the rabbis who, we are told, disagree in another *baraita*. This text claims that when a minority of the community sins, everyone brings a *chatat*, because the court is not responsible for a communal bull. If a majority transgresses, though, the congregation is not liable, because the court offers up a communal bull for all. This is the implication of the phrasing "from the people of the land"—the majority and even the entirety of the community. What sort of case does this *baraita* have in mind? If one thinks it might be an inadvertent action by any or all members of a community, then the court plays no role here. Why should it be obliged to bring a communal bull in a situation in which it issued no erroneous ruling? Maybe there was a mistaken court ruling, suggests Rav Yehudah again. But that, too, is impossible, because "from the people of the land" refers in our *baraita* to an inadvertent act committed without a mistaken court ruling.

These constructions are introduced by Rav Yehudah to clear away possible objections *après le fait*. This *must* be what the *baraita* means. If a minority of a community sins through inadvertence without a court ruling, each must offer a *chatat*, and the court doesn't compensate for them with a communal bull; perhaps one might conclude, though, that each of the members of a majority of the community that sins through inadvertence again without a mistaken court ruling is not liable to an individual *chatat*, because the court does bring a communal-bull offering when it issues an erroneous ruling. But, this would be wrong, and the Torah's phrase "from the people of the land" must be understood to mean that, even if a majority of the community errs and sins inadvertently, each and every one must bring a *chatat*, because no one was misinformed by the court (and this is key).

The *baraita* does allow for an individual (as long as he is part of a minority) who follows an erroneous court decision to bring a *chatat*. Rav Pappa doesn't buy it. Following the *baraita*, if a minority was misguided by a court ruling, then neither the community nor the court is required to bring an offering, the community because it followed the court and the court because it was a minority and thus shy of the majority requiring a communal bull. The Gemara takes Rav Pappa's understanding to be incorrect. Through some extremely fancy footwork, largely based not so much on the sources but more on the manner in which the *baraita* was argued, it comes to the conclusion that the members of a minority of a community who transgressed due to a court ruling must each bring a *chatat*; if there was no erroneous ruling but an inadvertent act, in that case as well they are responsible to bring a *chatat*. (Note that this is a different conclusion from our Mishnah.)

Rav Yehudah has now shown that the first *baraita* introduced here follows our Mishnah and, he argues, it is the work of R. Yehudah; the second *baraita*, he claims, disputes our Mishnah and is the work of the sages. The two *baraitot* disagree on the significant issue of if an individual who transgressed due to a mistaken court ruling is obliged to bring a *chatat*. But, the Gemara is not sure if the attributions of Rav Yehudah can hold water. Aren't both *baraitot* actually taught anonymously, with no statement of attribution in the first *baraita* to R. Yehudah and in the second to the rabbis. Maybe it's the opposite way around.

The Gemara begins its response as our *daf* comes to an end. The exclusionary terms mentioned above were constructed solely by R. Yehudah. Will this thesis hold water? Stay tuned.

HORAYOT 3

The previous *daf* concluded by claiming R. Yehudah was the one who developed the ideas from the Torah on exclusionary terms.

Our *daf* begins with him merely citing a passage in *Leviticus* (6:2) and identifying the text as "three exclusionary terms." Traditionally, the Talmud assumes that its readers have the entire Torah at their mental fingertips, so to speak, and this is an excellent example of that. Another argument to support the idea that R. Yehudah was responsible for the first *baraita* introduced in this string yesterday and the sages the second: In a Mishnah several *dapim* (sing. *daf* or Talmudic folio page) hence, R. Yehudah will be quoted as saying that the public and not the court brings a communal bull when a majority of the community sins.

Now, enter Rav Nachman to support the notion that the Mishnah's opening does represent unanimous agreement. He, too, channels Shmuel but states that it was R. Meir (not R. Yehudah) who argued that an individual who transgressed based on an erroneous court ruling is exempt from *chatat* liability, whereas the sages ruled that there was no exemption in such a case. When the Gemara asks for a little more detail, a *baraita* is introduced that makes this difference explicit, except that it refers not to an individual acting on an erroneous court ruling, but more vaguely that "the court ruled [incorrectly] and they acted." Who is this "they?" If "they" refers to the court, why would the rabbis hold them responsible, for that means a communal bull must be brought but the congregation has not even entered the picture here? The "they" must then refer to the community.

So, let us then say that the court issued an erroneous ruling, and the majority of the community acted in a way commensurate with this error. Must the court now bring a communal bull? How will R. Meir exempt the court from this standard issue communal-bull obligation? No, this won't work either.

Okay, then, maybe the court issued a mistaken ruling and a minority of the community followed its erroneous decision. R. Meir argues that an individual who sinned on this basis is free of *chatat* liability, whereas the sages argue that such an individual must bring a personal *chatat*. Rav Pappa, who seems to be trying to play spoiler but whose input has been repeatedly rejected, suggests that maybe, just maybe, both R. Meir and the sages agree that an individual who acts on an erroneous court ruling is not liable to offer a *chatat*. The point of disagreement, he avers, is rather whether the court members will tip the balance in the community to make it a majority, thus necessitating a communal bull. The sages say yes, and R. Meir says no.

A second elucidation of this *baraita* suggests that our case is one in which we have an erroneous court ruling which a majority of the community followed. The party responsible for the sages' position, the view poses, was R. Shimon who cites both the community and the court as liable for a communal bull. Thus, the "they" is both the court and the community. A third go at it: Maybe "they" refers to a tribe sinning in accordance with the court's ruling. Here it is R. Yehudah whose view was adopted by the sages, and a *baraita* we shall see in two *dapim* makes this case. A fourth and final effort—this one rather far-fetched, to say the least: Six tribes constituting the majority of the community's population overall sinned or seven tribes who do not constitute a demographic majority sinned. This view of the "they" is said to reflect the position of R. Shimon ben Elazar, and a *baraita* with exactly this line-up is cited, resulting in a communal-error bull. This last view is much clearer: Either a majority of the population or a majority of the tribes are sufficient to force a communal-error bull. In contrast to this view of the sages, R. Meir says we need both majorities to lead to a bull.

The Gemara now moves into an interesting discussion of how we constitute a "majority" of the Jewish people needed for a communal-error bull. Rav Assi says we need an absolute majority of the residents of the Land of Israel, implying that we do not count those living outside its borders. He cites a passage from *I Kings* (8:65) in which King Solomon, at the time of the Temple's dedication, called on "all Israel [to be] with him, a huge congregation." He then delimited the borders with geographic markers, and Rav Assi takes this to mean only Jews within these very borders and not outside them as constituting the "congregation."

Now, if a majority so constituted was misguided by a court ruling and later dwindled in number to become a minority, the issue of a communal bull revolves around a debate between R. Shimon and the rabbis (to be discussed several *dapim* hence). When a minority increases its numbers to become a majority, does the same difference of views come into play? Explication of this difference introduces some new Talmudic terminology concerning "awareness." Perhaps, R. Shimon would argue that there is communal-bull responsibility because he holds that the moment that awareness of *chatat* occurs, liability ensues; the rabbis follow the moment not of awareness but of transgression to ascertain *chatat* obligation and thus being a minority at that point no longer requires a communal bull. The Gemara wonders if the debate I have made a point of not introducing but which will surface on *daf* 10a is comparable. As it turns out, R. Shimon actually calls for both a moment of transgression and a moment of awareness when assessing *chatat* obligation. We shan't escape discussion of the other issue, but we shall but it off.

A small change of topics ensues with another hypothetical case: A court erroneously rules that some fat is allowed and a minority of the community consumes it. The court then becomes aware of its error, confesses as much, and reverses its judgment. Then, perhaps not the sharpest pin in the Jewish cushion, this same court again issues a ruling on the same kind of fat that it is allowed, and this time a different minority of the community follows them in consuming it, and again the court reverses its ruling. Not the most likely of scenarios, but as a possibility it must (apparently) be considered. Do these two minorities come together to form a majority and necessitate the offering of a communal bull? If we see these as two separate moments of awareness, perhaps they don't combine;

inasmuch as they both involve a kind of fat, however, perhaps they do.

Another thought along these same lines: Let us assume that the two minorities combine, because both rulings concerned a type of fat, and form a majority; if one minority ate a fat from one stomach of a ruminant, and another minority ate fat from the small intestine, what would the law be? Perhaps, the two fats do not combine because their prohibitions come from separate parts of the text of the Torah. Perhaps, by the same token, they do combine because both are forbidden fats.

Yet another thought along these same lines: If one minority transgressed a ruling concerned with forbidden fat, and another minority transgressed a ruling about consuming forbidden blood, what is the law? Perhaps, there is no combination because these are distinct prohibitions; perhaps, they do combine because both necessitate the same *chatat* sacrifice.

A fifth (and for now final) thought along these same lines: Assuming that both sins lead to *chatat* sacrifices and therefore they combine, then let's suppose one minority transgressed via a court ruling on forbidden fat and another sinned via an erroneous court ruling on idolatry. What is the law in this instance? Perhaps they don't combine because the prohibitions are distinctly different as are the sacrifices. Yet, perhaps they do combine because, if purposeful, their transgression would both lead to the same punishment of excision.

After all this truly interesting thinking, the Gemara decides to leave the matter unresolved: *teku*.

Okay, suppose then that a court ruled mistakenly that some forbidden fat was allowed and a minority of the community consumed it; then, the constituent members of that very court died. A different court was constituted and ruled in exactly the same erroneous manner as the first, now deceased, court; and a minority followed their ruling. Do these minorities combine to form a majority and bring on communal bull obligations for the errors? If it is the court that has to offer the communal bull, they no longer exist, at least not in this world. If the community is responsible for the bull, what is the law? Does the community as such still exist and need to bring the bull?

[a→b]

Or, maybe we need that first, now deceased, court to become aware of its erroneous ruling to force the bull. The Gemara concludes once again: *teku*.

More on the communal-error bull follows, and as noted earlier this always concerns the Great Sanhedrin. R. Yonatan asserts (oddly) that, if one hundred judges meet to offer a ruling and they judge mistakenly, all of them must do so to incur a communal-bull liability; that is, if there is so much as one dissenting judge, no communal bull is required. His prooftext is *Leviticus* 4:13, which speaks of "the entire community of Israel" (Alter: "all the community of Israel"). How does he get to one hundred from a court whose number is firmly set at seventy-one? Maybe this is simply hyperbole. Although it is ordinarily not allowed for the number of judges to increase, apparently it is okay if on a makeshift basis, but their number was always supposed to be odd, as opposed to even, so as to facilitate breaking a tie. R. Yonatan, then, does not sanction a communal bull in the case of a majority of the court erring; it must be the entire court. Rav Huna son of Rav Hoshaya agrees that "entire" (in the scriptural citation) seals the deal, as that word can have no other implication.

But, then again, maybe not. The Gemara now reiterates the entire first section of the Mishnah, noting that if a single judge or disciple realizes an erroneous court ruling but still goes along with the court, he is responsible for a *chatat*. This would seem to imply that, while the judge or disciple is liable for an offering, anyone else is exempt. But, if R. Yonatan's explanation is correct, the court's ruling could never take effect because it lacked unanimity.

Perhaps R. Yonatan got it wrong, or perhaps we have strayed too far from considerations concerning the communal-error bull.

A Mishnah to be introduced on the next *daf* is a bit more explicit in such instances. It discusses a court member who recognizes an error and confronts the entire court; and the court is exempt from a communal bull. The reason for the exception to liability must be that he spoke up rather than remaining silent with his dissent. If he had kept to himself, they would thus have incurred liability. Yet, despite not speaking up, silence apparently equals acquiescence (theoretically quite interesting in principle)—but silent dissent might also be manifest in a less than unanimous vote of the judges, thus averting communal bull liability.

At this point, Rav Mesharshiyya invokes a *baraita* to question R. Yonatan. It cites two great authorities, Rabban Shimon ben Gamliel and R. Elazar son of R. Tzadok, who claimed that we cannot impose a ruling on the people unless a majority of them have the capacity to follow it—in other words, no excessive demands should be placed on the populace at large. He develops this line by equating the majority with the entire nation of Israel. If a majority can enact a ruling, then it may be fitting for the entire people. This he takes to be a refutation (*teyuvta*) of R. Yonatan. And, the Gemara backs up his line of reasoning.

If R. Yonatan is wrong, the term "entire" is still there in *Leviticus* waiting to be expounded. The Gemara suggests it means that, if the "entire" court is in attendance, then its ruling is definitive; and if all seventy-one judges are not in attendance, their ruling is not definitive. Thus, all judges need not speak to a ruling, but they all have to be present. This answer seems to win the day.

The Gemara to this Mishnah ends on a homiletic note with a story from R. Yehoshua. If ten men judge, they all bear responsibility for a mistaken verdict, and this includes even disciples present at the time who do not confront (politely, of course) their teachers with evidence of their error. Silence in such a situation equals complicity in an erroneous decision, as we just saw above. Two practices reflecting this teaching are now told. When proceeding to court, Rav Huna always brought with him ten scholars, so that if he erred in judgment, he would have ten men to share the punishment with. When questions concerning if a slaughtered animal bore a fatal flaw came before Rav Ashi for judgment, he surrounded himself with ten expert butchers to help him rule as well as for the same reason as Rav Huna.

A new, lengthy Mishnah follows on material from the first one in this tractate. Case: The court allows something whose deliberate violation carries a punishment of excision, a majority of the populace follows the ruling, and then the court becomes aware of its error and withdraws its ruling. It is now liable to a communal-error bull. So, whether the court brought the bull or had not as yet done so, if someone who does not hear about the ruling's withdrawal goes and acts on the erroneous ruling, R. Shimon claims he is not liable to an individual *chatat*. R. Elazar is uncertain whether this person should bring a *chatat* for relying on his judgment or should not be so charged for relying on the court; thus, he must offer an *asham talui*, or suspended guilt offering, to cover himself within this realm of doubt.

R. Elazar tenders a little more detail on the nature of the doubt here and narrows its range of applicability. If our hypothetical person is at home throughout this erroneous ordeal, he is obliged to bring an *asham talui*. If, however, he was overseas, then R. Elazar agrees with R. Shimon that he is not so obliged. Just when you were hoping to gain clarity, R. Akiva states that, if the man went abroad, exemption seems more likely than liability. But Ben Azzai makes no such distinction as R. Elazar: at home or abroad makes no difference in his learned estimation. R. Akiva responds in the obvious manner: If this person was home, he had the opportunity to learn the court's decision, but being overseas he had no such opportunity.

The rest of this Mishnah, apparently unrelated to what has just preceded it, concerns cases in which court errors incur or do not incur communal bulls. It starts with three extraordinary possibilities of a court ruling to overturn an entire body of law, and which do not incur liability: If the court rules that the Torah provides no provision for *niddah* (a menstruant in the midst of her purification), Shabbat, or idolatry (rulings which border on complete impossibility). In these instances, the court would have been ruling to change everything about a given set of laws, but if it tried to change only one part of one of them, then it would be liable to a communal-error bull. An example: Yes, the court rules that there is *niddah* in the Torah, but one who enjoys conjugal relations at a prohibited time bears no responsibility for this; or, yes, there is provision for Shabbat in the Torah, but carrying from a private to a public domain is okay; or, yes, there is provision in the Torah against idolatry, but bowing down before an idol is okay. These three cases—all of them clearly transgressions—render the court liable for a communal-error bull. The Mishnah concludes with support drawn from an elliptical reference to the same passage in *Leviticus* (4:13)—"and a matter becomes obscure" (Alter: "and the thing be hidden [from the eyes of the assembly]")—a matter but not the entire body of law. I'm hoping the Gemara will help with this last difficult tidbit.

The Gemara begins with an explanation offered by Rav Yehudah channeling Rav of R. Shimon's reason for exempting someone who follows an erroneous court ruling even after the court has withdrawn its ruling. In a second rendition of Rav's explanation, he asserts that R. Shimon exempted the person because a ruling is only offered as a way of discriminating between an inadvertent and a purposeful offender.

The Gemara attempts to rebut R. Shimon's view exempting our "sinner" from *chatat* liability because he followed the court's ruling (even after it withdrew its decision). It refers to a case in which a communal bull was offered, and the person would have contributed in taxes to the fund for the communal bull. He would thus perforce have been apprised of the court's mistaken ruling. So, maybe the monies were collected without specifying that they were for a communal-bull fund. Or, maybe our "sinner" was out of town when the monies were collected.

Not surprisingly, other rabbis have views on this matter as well. As for our person who remains at home and still behaves in accordance with the ruling that the court has since withdrawn, a *baraita* teaches that R. Meir says he has incurred *chatat* liability; R. Shimon (as we know) exempts him; and R. Elazar is unsure; Sumchos claims the case is "ambiguous" (*talui*). How do these last two views differ: lack of certainty and ambiguity? R. Yochanan explains that R. Elazar requires an *asham talui*, but Sumchos does not. R. Zera tries to explain R. Elazar's reasoning with an actual case. A person inadvertently ate a piece of fat that might be forbidden and might be allowed, only later coming to this awareness; he is thus required to bring an *asham talui*.

HORAYOT 4

The last *daf* concluded in the middle of R. Zera's explanation of R. Elazar's *asham talui* ruling. Needless to say, if one says the community brings a communal bull, then that undoubtedly well known fact is sufficient to incur an *asham talui*. Even if one avers that it is the court that brings the bull, a considerably less well known fact publicly, there is enough evidence to warrant an *asham talui*. If he'd have asked, in other words, people would have told him.

That explains R. Elazar, and now on to Sumchos. The Gemara explains his view by means of a correspondence. Someone who violates the law because he was ignorant of a court's having withdrawn an erroneous ruling is like someone who offers his atoning sacrifice at twilight, which means there is doubt whether he offered it during the daytime (when it would be valid) or at nighttime (when it would not be). As a result, one does not incur an *asham talui*—it is simply "ambiguous."

In the Mishnah, R. Akiva argues that, if someone who traveling abroad followed the court's mistaken ruling, that person is exempt from an *asham talui*. Ben Azzai says it's all the same, at home or away. R. Akiva, as noted, explained that someone abroad would have no access to the information of the court's withdrawal, but someone at home might have heard about it or might not have—the former is exempt, while the latter incurs an *asham talui*. Praising R. Akiva's response, the Gemara apparently doesn't have Ben Azzai's subsequent reply (perhaps there was none), but it attempts to reason what it might have been. Rava suggests that "went overseas" refers to someone who had just set out but was still within the city limits when the court withdrew its erroneous ruling. Because he is technically still within the city, Ben Azzai would rule the need for an *asham talui*. R. Akiva, though, sees it differently—away from home is literally away, and he is thinking only of his impending trip, not assessing the latest ruling from the rabbinical court.

The Gemara now turns to the second part of the Mishnah at hand that had little, if anything at all, to do with the first half. This is the whole business of a court's ruling to repudiate entire bodies of law which leads to no communal bull. If the court made one of these outlandish rulings—e.g., there is no Shabbat prohibition in the Torah—one might easily surmise that a communal-error bull was in the offing, but the Torah also states the phrase "and a matter becomes obscured" (that cryptic phrase with which we hoped the Gemara would help). A *baraita* suggests that this implies just a "matter" and "not that an entire *mitzvah* becomes obscured" (that is, transgressed). Thus, all such cases of repudiating bodies of law are exempt from the bull.

So, what sorts of mistakes do compel a court to bring a communal-error bull? We had a look into this on the last *daf* when the text cited just this *baraita*: Not uprooting whole bodies of law but just parts ("a matter")—e.g., carrying from a private to a public domain on Shabbat—incurs communal bulls. Further dissection ensues. So, an entire body of law is exempt, and "an entire *mitzvah*" (contrasted above with "a matter") is as well. Maybe "a matter" should be understood as "an entire matter" which would insure that a communal-error bull would perforce be offered when an entire *mitzvah* "becomes obscured." No, it means that a detail from a *mitzvah* was somehow ignored.

How, the Gemara and all inquiring minds want to know, do we get to this conclusion? This will require a huge leap of academic faith. Ulla suggests that we take the final letter (*mem*) of the first word of our expression "and a matter become obscured" (*vene'lam davar*) and repeat it at the beginning of the second word, giving "and [some] of the matter becomes obscured" (*vene'lam midavar*). Chizkiyah offers a rather saner explanation: This phrase we have been working with must be read in connection with the next line in the Torah ("and they violate one of all the *mitzvot* of God"), and in that context it is clearly meant as part of a *mitzvah*, not an entire one. The rebuttal comes quickly: the term *mitzvot* is in the plural and hence implies at least two; thus, the transgression is one of two or more complete *mitzvot*, not a part or detail of one. Rav Nachman bar Yitzchak intervenes with a frankly lame suggestion that the word should be read not *mitzvot* but *mitzvat* (the singular, construct form of the noun)—remembering, of course, that the text is unpointed—but it is unclear if anyone takes this seriously. Yet another explanation now comes from Rav Ashi who locates a *gezerah shavah* (argument by analogy, see Glossary) between the word *davar* in our phrase and the same term in the Torah passage concerning the "rebellious sage" (*Deuteronomy* 17:8-11) which was cited two *dapim* back. In the latter, *davar* appears as *min-hadavar* (from the matter), and this (we are encouraged) is the way we should read our pesky phrase: a single matter, not an entire body of law.

In addition to the requirement that a mistaken court ruling not seek to repudiate an entire body of the law if we're looking for communal-error bull obligation, we now also learn that the court is exempt from a communal bull if they rule on a matter just as would the Sadducees. In other words, the Sadducees were so heterodox in their beliefs that, if a court ruled as they would, it is exempt. When the Gemara asks the simple question why, the response is curt and not terribly friendly: "Go read [about it] in the schoolhouse." Apparently, the Sadducees were so out of line with normative Judaism that not to understand why their rulings bordered on insanity was not to be up on the most basic of knowledge. One can't help thinking, though, that there must have been a nicer way to put it.

So, let's see now how the three examples given in the Mishnah for efforts to repudiate whole bodies of law work with this new condition. First, yes, the Torah certainly contains *niddah* prohibitions, and a communal-error bull is required for having conjugal relations during *niddah*. The proscription on the latter (*Leviticus* 15:28) is (more or less) clear, and even the bloody Sadducees follow this one (according to the Gemara, though no evidence is forthcoming). The Gemara now tries several ways to spin the answer about what sort of relations might be erroneously permitted by a court, and what the Sadducees would agree with.

Next we turn to the second question in the Mishnah: Yes, indeed, there are Shabbat prohibitions, but carrying from a private into a public domain is just fine. Such a mistaken statement incurs a communal bull. The law is clear here, so clear that even the Sadducees wouldn't violate it. Thus, there shouldn't be a communal-error bull obligation. Maybe, the Gemara suggests, the court erroneously ruled that carrying out from a private to a public domain is banned, but carrying in to a private domain is perfectly fine; or throwing from one domain to another is fine.

Let's move to the third arena: Yes, there is idolatry banned in the Torah, but bowing down to an idol is fine. This clearly is grounds for a communal-error bull. The Torah (*Exodus* 34:14) is explicit. Maybe, just maybe, the court ruled that bowing in the ordinary manner is banned, but when done in a manner out of the ordinary vis-à-vis the idol in question, it's allowed.

[a→b]

Abrupt change of subject back to the initial point that the mistaken court ruling not repudiate a whole body of Torah law. Rav Yosef lobs a softball—Is there a communal-bull obligation if the court rules that during Shabbat there's no ban on plowing, one of the basic thirty-nine categories of labor explicitly prohibited on Shabbat? Is this a whole body of law (the plowing prohibition) or just one of thirty-nine categories? The Gemara attempts to answer this query by reiterating the same three Mishnah cases just reiterated to demonstrate that sex during *niddah*, Shabbat carrying, and bowing to an idol constitute entire legal bodies, but each are brushed aside as "details" of a larger legal corpus.

No answer directly coming to Rav Yosef's question, the Gemara cites a parallel question from R. Zera: Is there a communal-bull obligation if the court mistakenly rules that there is no law against working the land during the Sabbatical year (the seventh year in cycle during which the land must remain fallow)? The text explains how the court might have made such an error and asks if this constitutes a full body of law or only a part (for we till the soil the other six years as part of the seven-year, Sabbatical cycle).

As the Gemara to this Mishnah comes to a close, Ravina interjects something of an answer to this belabored set of queries. He cites a *baraita* that invokes capital punishment for a prophet who prophesies the repudiation of something from the Torah. If such a prophet were to prophesy the abolition of part of a *mitzvah* (with the exception of idol worship) and the perpetuation of part, R. Shimon declares that he escapes the death penalty. Idolatry is a different matter altogether—if he says it's okay to bow down today to it and repudiate it tomorrow, he gets the death penalty. Therefore, claiming that there is no ban on labor during the Sabbatical year is a partial nullification and a partial continuation. One can understand more fully now the wrath of opponents of Shabbatai Zvi (1626-1676), the false Messiah, in the seventeenth century. Oddly, it was the Muslims who presented him with the choice of the death penalty or conversion, not the Jews, though if the Sanhedrin (even with its renowned reluctance to impose capital punishment) had been in place at the time, he might easily have been executed by his own people.

On to a new Mishnah with more on communal-error bulls. This one we caught a glimpse of earlier. There is no communal-error bull in any of the following scenarios: A court makes a mistaken ruling, and one of the judges becomes aware of the error and tells his fellow judges that they have "erred"; or the most eminent member of the court (*rosh yeshivah*) is absent; or any one of the judges was a convert, a *mamzer* (the child of an adulterous or incestuous coupling), a *natin* (a descendant of Gibeonites who signed a peace treaty under false pretenses with Joshua at the time of the conquest of Canaan, and Joshua kept his word to accept them but relegated them to the status of woodchoppers and water-bearers); or an elder incapable of siring children. Details will follow in the Gemara.

We have had part of this already explained, and the reason for requiring the presence of the most eminent court member will be elucidated in the Gemara. A *gezerah shavah* is hauled out to help with the rest of the Mishnah. In short, all members of the "assembly" (*edah*, the key term found in two spots, one concerning the communal-error bull and one concerning capital punishment) must be able to rule properly or they do not incur communal-bull obligations.

The Gemara begins with the case of the court's most celebrated figure. How do we know that his presence is essential for a communal-error bull exemption? Rav Sheshet explains on the basis of a teaching from R. Yishmael's academy. The sages claimed that if a court issued a ruling to which even the benighted Sadducees agree, then the court is exempt from a communal bull, the reason being that they were negligent and should have studied such a relatively easy matter more thoroughly. Similarly, if the most illustrious member of the court is absent, an erroneous court ruling is not subject to a communal bull, because they should have waited for their star's return and studied the matter more thoroughly under his more expert guidance. As the *gezerah shavah* cited in the Mishnah and reiterated here puts it, the court must be "fit to rule." What's the problem with the list of excluded types (*mamzer*, *natin*, convert, and elder incapable of siring children)? The justification, given by Rav Chisda, is a bit odd, but it harks backs to Moses' establishment of the initial Sanhedrin (*Numbers* 11:16) where he called for seventy men to "stand there [the Tent of Meeting] with you" (Alter: "station themselves there with you"). The term "with you" is taken to mean "like Moses" and thus implying free of any genealogical imperfection. That explanation is quickly junked, and Rav Nachman bar Yitzchak claims a different verse as the source. Earlier (*Exodus* 18:22), Yitro counseled Moses to name judges who "shall bear it with you." Here "with you" more seamlessly fits the "like you" mold, and the Gemara offers no objection.

Quickly on to another Mishnah, and in this one we get erroneous court decisions, sinning communities, and what the law is in each instance. The court inadvertently rules erroneously and the community also inadvertently follows the ruling: communal-error bull. The court purposefully rules erroneously and the community follows suit inadvertently: each sinning individual brings a personal *chatat* (a ewe or female goat), but no communal bull. The court rules inadvertently and the community follows its ruling purposefully, no offering of any sort is required.

The Gemara here is relatively brief. It starts with the last case and assumes that the community's exemption was due to its purposeful transgression. How, the Gemara asks, are we to conceive of an inadvertent sin that resembles a purposeful one? If a court mistakenly ruled that some forbidden fat is allowed and someone came along and confused a piece of such fat with a piece of allowable fat, and accidentally ate the forbidden piece, you have just such a case. An individual *chatat* is called for here. A further complication with the Mishnah follows, but it is quickly resolved and not of legal significance.

Our *daf* ends with the first parts of another Mishnah concerned with just who is responsible for bringing a communal-error bull. R. Meir rules as follows. The court offers a mistaken ruling and the entire community (or most of its constituent members) follows suit: the court, not the community, is obligated to bring a bull. However, if the court allows for pagan practice, then it must bring both a bull and a male goat; the community brings neither. R. Yehudah disagrees. In his view, each of the twelve tribes brings a communal-error bull. In the case of allowing for idol worship, each tribe offers up a bull and a male goat; the court gets off scot free.

HORAYOT 5

We begin this new *daf* in the middle of a Mishnah discussing who is responsible for bringing the communal-error bull when the court rules mistakenly and the majority or entirety of the community acts according. Some of this has already been previewed on the previous three *dapim*. R. Shimon offers a unique opinion: Each of the twelve tribes brings a communal bull and the court brings a thirteenth. If it's a case of allowing pagan practice, ratchet up the penalty to thirteen bulls and thirteen male goats, one of each for each tribe and for the court.

Another case: The court rules erroneously, and either a majority (seven) of the tribes or a majority of the constituents of each of those seven tribes behaves accordingly. R. Meir rules that the court brings a bull; if the ruling involves idol worship, it's a bull and a male goat. R. Yehudah has a different take on this. If seven tribes transgress the law, each brings a communal bull; and—here's the interesting difference—each of the other tribes also brings a bull because of their seven sinning tribal brethren. The Mishnah then reiterates that even the non-transgressors must make offerings owing to those who did transgress the law. Thus, there should always be twelve communal-error bulls offered. This ruling takes the idea of "community" or communal responsibility seriously, to say the least.

Meanwhile, R. Shimon has yet another view. In such an instance in which seven of the tribes transgress, he opines that each of them offers up a bull and an eighth must be brought by the court. In a case of idol worship mistakenly sanctioned by the court, it's eight bulls and eight male goats. Unlike R. Yehudah, he argues that only the sinning tribes, as well as the court, bring offerings.

How do we get to a situation calling for a communal-error sacrificial offering? R. Yehudah argues as follows. One tribe's high court might offer an erroneous decision and members of the tribe transgress on the basis of it. The tribe must then bring a communal bull, but the other tribes are off the hook. The sages disagree, saying that communal bulls are only brought when the Great Sanhedrin, the court of seventy-one judges, rules mistakenly and leads to sinning behavior. Individual tribal high courts cannot trigger communal bulls. The prooftext (*Leviticus* 4:13) speaks of the "entire community [or assembly, that is, the court] of Israel makes an error," not the "assembly" of a single tribe.

Lots of material to work with here, and it will keep us busy right through to the end of this first chapter of tractate *Horayot*. Rather than begin by addressing the text of the Mishnah, the Gemara starts with a *baraita* that adds to the overall picture. The court rules erroneously concerning one forbidden item and the community sins accordingly as well as in another area. The court then realizes that it had erred but is in doubt about which of the two areas it had mistakenly allowed. Perhaps the court is obliged to bring a communal-error bull, but the scriptural text (*Leviticus* 4:14) explicitly states: "When the sin [not the sinner] becomes known" (Alter: "When the offense that they committed become known"). So, a bull is offered only when the specific transgression itself is known.

The biblical text just cited goes on to speak of the "sin which they transgressed." Because the last three words here (in translation) aren't necessary for the Bible to make its point (commission of a sin *is* a transgression), they must have another import, and the Gemara takes this to be that each tribe that sinned must bring its own communal bull. One might think that the text is speaking of individuals sinning and individuals accordingly bringing bulls, but the Gemara makes clear that the Torah speaks specifically of "the community" (*hakahal*). Virtually by definition, individuals do not bring communal-error bulls.

The *baraita* goes on to explain the passage from the Mishnah about seven tribes sinning, as R. Yehudah understood it. In that case, seven bulls, one from each of seven tribes, are required, and all the other tribes, too, must bring a communal bull. Why? The biblical text speaks of "the community"—it's a community obligation once the numbers reach seven, a majority of the whole. R. Shimon offers a second opinion: eight bulls, one from each of the sinning seven tribes and one from the court. How does he get to this stance? He employs a *gezerah shavah* linking "the community" in this passage with the same term in the previous verse. In the latter, the text speaks of "the eyes of the community" which, he claims, means the court; he then suggests it might have the same meaning in the expression under discussion here. Result: The court, too, brings a separate (the eighth) communal bull.

As is often the case, R. Meir has yet another view. If a majority of the tribes transgresses the law, only the court (not the tribes themselves) brings a communal-error bull. He uses the same *gezerah shavah* as R. Shimon to reach this understanding. The focus on "the community" meaning the court here leads him to assert that only the court must bring a bull. The *baraita* ends with a ruling of R. Meir, channeled through R. Shimon ben Elazar: If six tribes whose constituents make up a majority of the community of Israel or seven tribes whose members do not constitute an overall majority transgress the law, the court brings a communal bull.

Just above the *baraita* distinguished between the scriptural text's "when the sin becomes known" and knowledge of who the sinners were becoming known. As we often see, the Gemara first wants to know who, which Tanna, issued this opinion. It's not R. Eliezer, because he has ruled elsewhere (*Keretot* [Excisions] 19a) that, if someone transgresses a proscription but is not sure which proscription, he is obliged to offer up a *chatat*. It is interesting that the Gemara would take the time to start answering the question "who" by declaring "who it is not." As presented in the Gemara, R. Eliezer's ruling seems to have little to do with communal bulls, but that would be a rush to judgment. If an individual transgresses a proscription but doesn't know which one, R. Eliezer calls for a *chatat*; thus, he would argue that a communal error (by the court) would necessitate a communal bull. Rav Ashi now interjects that maybe R. Eliezer's view actually does jibe with the *baraita*. R. Eliezer may require a personal *chatat* for a violation, even if it is not precisely known, but it's different with communal violations. In the latter instance, the precise sin must be known. This string is left off with a brief debate about prepositions in the biblical text.

Still focused on the *baraita* which immediately followed the last Mishnah, the Gemara now wants to know how it reached the conclusions that it did. R. Yehudah notes that the term *kahal* (community, congregation) appears four times in the section of the Torah dealing with communal bulls (*Leviticus* 4:13-14). Twice it is prefixed with the definite article (hence, *hakahal*, or "the community") which R. Yehudah considers superfluous and hence available for exegesis. So, here is how he explains all four: 1. one to compel a communal-bull offering from each community; 2. one to inform us that the mistaken ruling is the court's fault and the forbidden behavior is the community's; 3. one to inform us that the other tribes, those that did not transgress, nonetheless get "dragged" along with the sinning ones; and 4. one to see that any tribe that followed its own court's erroneous ruling must also offer up a communal bull.

That was R. Yehudah's take on the *baraita*. We turn now to R. Shimon who sees only three instances of *kahal*. He sees the fourth being beyond the scope of exegesis, because the definitive particle in one of the two cases of *hakahal* is not superfluous but ordinary (and necessary) biblical usage. One of the three usable instances is there to compel a communal-bull offering from each community; the other two form a *gezerah shavah* for elucidation, teaching ultimately that both court and community must offer up a communal-error bull.

On to R. Meir's thinking, and he is the most delimiting in his exegesis. He refuses to make anything unusual of the definite article in the two instances of *hakahal*. That leaves him with two instances to expound. He, too, reads them as a *gezerah shavah*, but the conclusion at which he arrives is different from R. Shimon. He concludes that the court, not the community, brings a bull.

R. Shimon ben Elazar relayed a ruling of R. Meir at the end of the *baraita* about constituting a majority. Through a cryptic reading of *Numbers* 15:24 concerning an inadvertent transgression, two passages therein seem to have conflicting messages, but R. Shimon uses this to explain as follows: Be it six tribes whose constituents constitute a majority of the overall community of Israel or seven tribes whose total members may not constitute a majority of the population, they perforce bring a communal-error bull.

[a→b]

Remembering that R. Shimon and R. Meir both used two instances of *kahal* for a *gezerah shavah*, and R. Shimon used his third and remaining instance to compel a bull for every transgressing tribe, that leaves no instance for them to compel the court to offer a bull. How do they go about expounding that? Abaye explains that the verse concerning inadvertent commission of a sin by the community is stated in the passive voice—implying the sin was due to other forces, which has to be the court and its erroneous ruling; the transgressors were the community. Rava chimes in with another scriptural verse (*Numbers* 15:26) which reaches the same conclusion. Do we need both Abaye's and Rava's sources to explain this ruling? Of course, we do. The Talmud almost always raises this profoundly rhetorical question and proceeds to demonstrate that each text provides only one part of the solution; it also notes what we might have ignored or how we might have erred had we only had one or the other source to substantiate our case. This string ends with a reminder that the case we have been expounding concerns the communal bull for erroneous rulings with respect to idol worship. Via another *gezerah shavah*, the text analogizes that the same ruling applies to other communal transgressions as well.

At the end of the lengthy Mishnah with which we began our *daf*, there was mention of the high court or courts of individual tribes rendering mistaken rulings. R. Yehudah asked if all the tribes must bring communal bulls if only one sinned on the basis of an erroneous ruling of the Great Sanhedrin. Perhaps when seven tribes (a majority) transgressed the law, all tribes must bring a bull, but if only one sinned, there's no liability. On the other hand, perhaps the number makes no difference—if one or more transgress, all pay the price in bulls. The Gemara inserts at this point an extremely brief *baraita* in an effort to answer this question; it is a question concerning what must be brought as a communal sacrifice, and it answers one bull, with R. Shimon stating two bulls. At first glance, this new *baraita* hardly clarifies anything. What is being debated? It has to be where a single tribe sinned, and R. Shimon would require one bull each from the tribe and the court. But, what sort of ruling did the single tribe in question transgress? It has to be a ruling of the

Great Sanhedrin, because R. Shimon rules out a tribal high court's decision triggering a communal bull. So, we have a single tribe sinning on the basis of an erroneous ruling of the Great Sanhedrin. Who would have been the authority to offer such a view? It can't be R. Meir or R. Shimon. It must be R. Yehudah. If only one tribe transgresses the law, that tribe and it alone brings a bull—no "dragging" the other tribes into the area of bull obligation.

But, wait...there's another possibility here. Maybe, our short and cryptic *baraita* was referring to a case in which not one but six tribes transgressed, and the ruling thus follows the view articulated by R. Shimon ben Elazar. Throw out the entire explanation, and let's try again.

Another *baraita* is now introduced. In it we find that R. Yehudah claims that, if a single tribe sins on the basis of a mistaken ruling of its own high court, the tribe must bring a bull, but the other tribes are exempt (no dragging). If the sinning tribe acted on the basis of a mistaken ruling of the Great Sanhedrin, though, all the other non-sinning tribes are also obligated to bring a bull. This *baraita* clearly, succinctly, and in short order resolves the initial query—one can only wonder why the Gemara saw fit to take us through the circuitous argumentation of the previous *baraita*.

Rav Ashi informs us that a close reading of the final lines of the Mishnah in question would lead to the same conclusion. The Mishnah stated that if one tribe sins on the basis of its high court's erroneous ruling, it must bring a bull and no other tribe is so obligated. The Gemara explains: Why mention this last clause? Isn't it implied in the previous one? Once we state that the sinning tribe is obligated to bring a bull, the implication is clear that no other tribes are. Nothing, of course, is really superfluous—perhaps on the surface but never in substance. The subliminal message to be teased out of this apparent superfluity is that when a tribe sins on the basis of a ruling of the Great Sanhedrin—as opposed to that tribe's own high court—then, all the other tribes are dragged into it. This was, after all, the message from the start.

Now, what was R. Shimon's view in a case in which one tribe transgresses the law based on a ruling of the Great Sanhedrin? Do they bring a communal offering? Once again, our cryptic *baraita* is rallied to the cause: What is the communal offering brought? One bull, states the Tanna of the *baraita*; two bulls, says R. Shimon. The Gemara takes this apart as it did in the earlier instance with R. Yehudah's thinking. It concludes that we must be dealing with the case of a single tribe and an erroneous ruling of the Great Sanhedrin. If this reconstruction is on the mark, then R. Shimon calls for a communal bull when a single tribe transgresses. As above, though, the Gemara proceeds to brush this demonstration aside, and again it turns to the Mishnah itself. There it said plainly that the "sages" ruled a single tribe obligated to bring a bull if it based its sinning behavior on a mistaken ruling of the Great Sanhedrin. The text then proceeds to unpack "sages" and explains that they represent the views of R. Shimon. Q.E.D.

With these cases closed, the Gemara segues laterally to ask how R. Yehudah and R. Shimon know that one tribe may be called a "community" (or "congregation," *kahal*) in the Tanakh. From *II Chronicles* 20:5, our two rabbis must have made this association. In the citation from this passage, there is mention of "the new Courtyard," and the Gemara now digresses to ask what this term might mean. The Gemara cites R. Yochanan who claims it means the Temple Mount. Before this can be debated, though, R. Acha bar Yaakov jumps back to disagree that the citation from *II Chronicles* actually refers to a single tribe; he says in the instance cited it must be two. Instead, he locates another source (*Genesis* 48:4) for the association of a single tribe with a community; the biblical text refers specifically to the tribe of Benjamin as a "congregation." But, we're not done with challenges yet.

Disputing this conclusion, one infrequently heard from scholar, Rav Shaba, suggests that maybe the phrasing of this passage only means that, with the birth of Benjamin, the twelve tribes will be complete and constitute a community. Thus, the term refers not to the tribe of Benjamin but to all of them together. His interlocutor, Rav Kahana, doesn't buy it: Oh, only twelve tribes make a community but not eleven—nonsense! When God assured Jacob in our prooftext that he'd have a community, He meant Benjamin, proving finally that a single tribe can a community make.

R. Meir has argued that only the court is obliged to offer up a communal-error bull. But, there is a *baraita* that throws doubt on this view. It quotes R. Shimon on the topic of the two bulls brought to the Temple's inauguration by the Leviim and contrasts two passages from *Numbers* (8:8 and 8:12) about what those bulls were actually for. The *daf* ends in the middle of a sentence of the Gemara. We shall pick up this trail on the next *daf*.

HORAYOT 6

Our new *daf* picks up in the middle of a *baraita*, citing a passage from *Ezra* (8:35) about the return of the Jewish people from exile in Babylonia to the Land of Israel. Among the many offerings they brought were twelve bulls and twelve male goats (for the twelve tribes), although the text declares all of the offerings together to be an *olah* (burnt offering) and not a *chatat* (sin offering). They can't be the same. The *baraita* resolves this by saying that all these offerings are like an *olah* in that neither *olah* nor *chatat* are consumed by humans. It would thus seem that the second bull mentioned as a *chatat* in the *Numbers* verse on the previous *daf* is not consumed. All of these offerings appear to be communal offerings made in the wake of a transgression involving idol worship. If, then, twelve is the expected number of male goats, the differing reasoning of R. Yehudah (if all tribes sin, each brings one; if only a majority, the other are "dragged" along) and R. Shimon (if eleven tribes sin, each brings one, as does the court for a total of twelve) can each find a way to jibe with the text. However, R. Meir only requires the court to bring an offering, and it appears difficult for him to come up with twelve. The Gemara gives the only possible answer: The sinners sinned, then continued sinning for a total of twelve times, though they must have repented in between each time. Each idolatrous transgression required an offering.

One of the prooftexts cited by the Gemara concerned *chatat* offerings brought by the exiles returning from Babylonia to expiate the much earlier sins of the generation of Tzidkiyahu, the last king of Judah. The Gemara now asks how this can have been so, because those who practiced pagan rituals at the time of Tzidkiyahu had died by the time of the return to the Land. No *chatat* may be offered on behalf of a deceased person. Rav Pappa claims that the rule about no *chatat* offerings for the dead was for individual *chataot*, but there is no such rule for communal *chataot*.

This would be a good resolution, but the Gemara wants a source that allows for descendants to bring *chataot* for their antecedents. First, it proposes a verse from *Psalms* (45:17) which suggests that the descendants of transgressors can offer atonement for their forebears. But, it quickly rejects this verse, because it could just as well be used to justify an individual descendant bringing a *chatat* for a dead relative. Next, it suggests that Rav Pappa's explanation may be compared with the monthly *chatat* of a male goat that was sacrificed for *tumah* (impurities) transgressions; the money for these goats came from a communal fund in the Temple treasury. Indeed, some of the contributors to the fund would have passed on by the time the money for a new goat was expended and the goat sacrificed. But, the Gemara rejects this line of reasoning as well, because it remains within the realm of possibility that none of the contributors to the fund for male goats had died at the time a goat was offered in sacrifice. This is altogether different from the case of the Babylonian returnees whose offerings long postdated the actual transgressors.

Let's try a third source for Rav Pappa. This time we get a biblical citation (*Deuteronomy* 21:8) concerning atonement via the decapitated calf (*eglah arufah*) for the entire generation from Egypt. The opportunity for exegesis here involves superficially superfluous language in the text. As thus construed, the ritual of the decapitated calf serves to atone for that much earlier generation; thus, communal *chatat* offerings by descendants may atone for the transgression of their deceased predecessors. Or, maybe not: Those who take part in the ritual of the decapitated calf are, of course, all alive and all intended beneficiaries of the ritual; it is also intended to atone for the deceased. Our original case of the generation of Tzidkiyahu, though, involved only dead people being atoned for. But, wait, when the exiles returned to the Land, many helped build the Second Temple, according to Ezra. That these survivors were still living at the time of the atonement means that they, too, were beneficiaries. Maybe, suggests the Gemara, those survivors were only a minority of people who returned from exile, but in actuality it would seem that they constituted a majority. Again, the reference is to *Ezra* (3:13) wherein we find that some people cried and some celebrated, with the former drowning out the latter; the Gemara takes the former to be those who survived from the First Temple's destruction, with the latter being those born afterward.

Now, there is another problem with the transgressors from the time of King Tzidkiyahu. They were purposeful transgressors, and no *chatat* can ever serve to absolve them. This time the discussion is brief. They received a special, anomalous dispensation—despite deliberately having transgressed the law. The proof offered is the nature of the list and numbers of animals brought to sacrifice, which is out of the ordinary.

Getting back to our Mishnah, there is a difference of views about who brings the communal bull, the court or the community.

A *baraita* is introduced for a case in which we have an erroneous court ruling and a community that followed the ruling in action. Now, if a member of the community dies after the transgression but before the bull is offered, "they" are still obliged to bring a bull; if a member of the court dies before the bull is offered, "they" are not so obliged.

Before we can even begin to take this *baraita* apart, the Gemara demands to know who issued it. One string of rabbis suggests R. Meir because of his—by now well known—view that the court, not the community, brings the communal bull. Let's see how this will work. R. Meir would interpret both instances of "they" (in both cases represented not by the pronoun but by third-person plural verbs in Hebrew) as the court; if a member of the community dies, "they" (the court) bring the bull. If a member of the court dies, "they" (the court) do not, because the court's offering is a *chatat*, not a communal offering, and when one of the parties to the *chatat* dies, the obligation disappears.

Rav Yosef doesn't buy this ascription of the *baraita* to R. Meir. He sees it as representing the view of R. Shimon who argues that the court and the community together bring the communal-error bull. So, if one member of the community dies, "they" (court and community) must together bring a bull; a community *chatat* obligation survives any number of deaths within the community. If a member of the court dies, though, "they" (here meaning only the court) is not obliged, because with the death of one of its members, the *chatat* of multiple parties (members of the court) no longer applies. Abaye finds this problematic, and he cites yet another *baraita* to prove that R. Shimon held the opposite view that, even if a member of the court died, it still was obliged to bring a bull. Here's how this *baraita* goes. The bull and male goat set aside for the special Yom Kippur sacrifices were misplaced, so the Temple official set others aside in their stead. The latter animals were sacrificed, and then the original two were discovered. R. Yehudah rules that the two must be left to die, for the communal *chatat* is like a personal *chatat*: the original beast must die, even if atonement has been achieved through substitutes. R. Elazar and R. Shimon claim that the original animals should be allowed to graze until they develop blemishes—making them no longer serviceable as offerings—and then sell them. Thus, as they see it, a communal *chatat* is not left to die and thus does not resemble a personal *chatat*. R. Shimon would thus argue that a *chatat* held by more than one party is not treated in the same manner as a personal *chatat*, and refutes Rav Yosef's rendition of R. Shimon's views on the matter.

To explain further, the Yom Kippur bull works to atone only for the priestly class; it is not a communal *chatat* but a partnership *chatat*, and R. Shimon rules that it not be left to die but to graze, develop a blemish, and then be sold. Legally, a partnership *chatat* in his view is like a communal *chatat*, and the court is like a band of partners; if one of them dies, the others are obliged to bring the *chatat* just like a communal *chatat*. Thus, Rav Yosef's rendition of his views can't be right, according to Abaye.

Rav Yosef responded to Abaye that the priestly class is not like any old band of partners, nor is their Yom Kippur bull any old partnership *chatat*. They constitute a "community" (citing *Leviticus* 16:33 where they are referred to as a *kahal*). From the biblical text, he argues that this offering is like a communal *chatat*; if the priestly class gains atonement with a substitute bull, as per R. Shimon, the original is not left to die. In other cases of a partnership *chatat*, such as the court's communal-error bull, R. Shimon would concur that they be dealt with like personal *chataot*.

[a→b]

Now the Gemara has some doubts about the way Rav Yosef has construed things to this point. If the priestly class constitutes a community, they would bring their own communal bull in the case of a mistaken ruling. If they do, then there will be not twelve tribes bringing a total of twelve bulls (as R. Shimon indicated) but thirteen (one each from the twelve tribes and one from the Kohanim or priests). Thus, the Kohanim cannot constitute a separate community. R. Acha son of R. Yaakov now offers a kind of compromise solution. Yes, the priestly class (the Kohanim) is a community, but it does not bring a communal-error bull. Kohanim are part of the tribe of Levi, and the Levites do not constitute a community. How does he get to this conclusion? A citation from *Genesis* 48:4 notes that only a tribe with a "possession" in the Land can be dubbed a community (*kahal*), but a tribe without a "possession" cannot; the Levites have no possession in the Land, and hence are not a community, and hence they cannot bring a communal-error bull. Being part of the Levites, the Kohanim are in the same boat. Thus, when the priestly class brings a bull on Yom Kippur, it is like a communal offering.

The Gemara wonders if the Levites really aren't obligated to bring a bull. If in line with an erroneous court ruling, all the tribes transgress and must bring bulls, there will then be only eleven, and R. Shimon designated the figure at twelve. Thus, he must consider the Levites a community and bull-worthy, meaning that Rav Acha son of R. Yaakov's view that the tribe of Levi is no community can't be correct. Abaye to the rescue, pointing to the next verse in *Genesis* where Jacob tells his beloved son Joseph that the latter's two famous sons, Efrayim and Menasheh, will be like his own sons Reuven and Shimon; that would mean that the tribe of Joseph is in fact to be treated as two tribes. So, even if the Levites are not required to pony up with a communal bull, there will be twelve.

Nice try, avers Rava (citing the next *Genesis* verse, 48:6) as he rejects Abaye's reasoning. The Bible says that Efrayim and Menasheh are to be regarded as on a par with Jacob's sons *only* regarding their inheritance; the implication (more like an extrapolation) is that they are not two distinct tribes, and if Levi brings no bull, there will only be eleven. R. Shimon insisted on twelve, meaning Levi has to count as a community and has to bring a bull when required.

This constitutes another repudiation of Rav Yosef, for if the priests constitute a community, we will have thirteen bulls, should the entire people transgress. Thus, the Kohanim are not a community and thus do not offer up a bull on their own; the Levites do bring their own communal bull. In sum, their Yom Kippur bull sacrifice is not a communal one.

This is all getting fairly arcane. The Gemara doesn't accept the way Rava dismissed the suggestion of Efrayim and Menasheh as two separate tribes. It notes that they had distinct banners in the tribal encampment in the desert. So, their distinctiveness was not *only* a matter of inheritance, and may easily have extended to offering communal bulls. But, inheritance and encampments were not sharply separable—both came from Jacob—and hence, while Efrayim and Menasheh were regarded as distinct in these two arenas, that's it. As it often does, the Gemara offers a second argument here: Efrayim and Menasheh had separate banners to maintain the high reputation of the balanced encampment; otherwise the two were not distinct. The Gemara tries once more: When the princes of each tribe (*Nesiim*) brought commemorative offerings at the inauguration of the Mishkan (Tabernacle), Efrayim and Menasheh are listed as doing so separately. Again, nice try, for this was only to honor the princes, we are told, rather than to choose one of them over the other. The separation did not extend beyond that as far as communal-error bulls.

Apparently, even the Gemara is getting tired of this discussion and now returns to the more central question of what a partnership *chatat* is. Did R. Shimon consider it comparable to a communal *chatat*, as claimed by Abaye, or not? A *baraita* is introduced in which R. Shimon lists five types of *chatat* that must be left to die: (1) the offspring of a *chatat* conceived after being designated as such, which takes on its mother's sanctity but can't be offered because it was not designated as such; (2) the *temurah* (exchanged animal to be offered) of a *chatat*, consecrated like a *chatat* but not offerable; (3) a *chatat* whose owner dies before being offered; (4) a *chatat* whose owners gain atonement via a substitute *chatat* when the original animal designated is misplaced; (5) and a *chatat* that is allowed to grow to more than one year of age, the legal limit.

So, let's take this apart. (1) can't apply to a communal *chatat*, because communities only designate male animals; (2) similarly doesn't the fit the bill because a *temurah* is only for individuals, not communities; and (3) won't work because a community can't die. So, that eliminates three possibilities. Rulings on (4) and (5) may qualify as cases in which the animals need be left to die. If one wanted to disprove their applicability, one would have to argue an analogy with one of the three dismissed cases. However, doing so would be to derive the possible from the impossible, the applicable cases from the inapplicable ones. The three instances ruled out were consequences of impossible scenarios; the two remaining ones can exist.

As the first chapter of our tractate comes to a close, the Gemara replies that the five cases laid out by R. Shimon as articulated in the *baraita* all come from a single set of circumstances. Thus, R. Shimon was not trying to extract something possible from something impossible. He was only explaining the contours of the law as he had learned it. Thus, if any of these cases is impractical, as with a communal *chatat*, the entire law regarding all five is inapplicable. Inasmuch as (1) and (2) cannot exist in a partnership *chatat*, the law regarding all five, the full set, is irrelevant. If one of the parties involved in a *chatat* should die before it is sacrificed, the *chatat* is not left to die, a view consonant with that of Abaye who constructed R. Shimon's views in this fashion.

Chapter Two

The Anointed Priest Ruled (*dapim* 6b-9b)

HORAYOT 6B (CONTINUED)

We now move to the second chapter of this tractate which deals with a special set of laws concerning the *chatat* offered by the Anointed Priest (*Kohen mashiach*) and contrasts them with the laws of the communal-error bull we have thus far been discussing. It will also look at the *chatat* offered by the Nasi, and how it differs from that of a commoner and the Anointed Priest.

The Mishnah begins by pointing to a situation requiring the Anointed Priest to bring a *chatat*. If he were without purposeful intent to issue a mistaken ruling and then transgress on its basis inadvertently, he is obliged to bring a bull *chatat*. If he without purposeful intent issued a mistaken ruling and then purposefully transgressed on its basis, or if he purposefully ruled erroneously and then transgressed without purposeful intent, no *chatat* need be brought. Explanation: the rulings that the Anointed Priest makes for himself are similar to the rulings issued by a court for the community.

The Gemara begins by asking why we need the first sentence of the Mishnah. Unintentional mistaken rulings and unintentional transgressions obviously lead to a bull. Nothing in the text of the Mishnayot, though, is ever unnecessary or superfluous, only superficially so. Abaye explains that the case at hand is one in which the Anointed Priest ruled mistakenly and then forgot why he had made the error. When he transgressed the law, he stated that he was acting on the basis of his own ruling. So, in such an instance, we need to know that a communal-error bull is required. Otherwise, we might think him an intentional transgressor, and there is no bull required for purposeful sinning—the penalty lies elsewhere.

The latter part of the Mishnah offers two scenarios leading to exemptions from bull offerings. Now, the Gemara would like a source. As our *daf* comes to a close, we get the beginning of a *baraita* which cites the Torah (*Leviticus* 4:3) from which passage we are to associate the Anointed Priest with the community as far as obligations to a *chatat* are concerned. Maybe, the *baraita* goes on, we don't need a scriptural source because logic could do the trick just as well. This may be the first instance in this tractate of logic and scripture coming together to reach a conclusion.

HORAYOT 7

The previous *daf* ended by suggesting that logic, in addition to scripture, might also deem that the Anointed Priest be regarded in the same fashion as the community. How so? Well, the *chatat* brought by a community as well as that brought by the Anointed Priest both differ from the *chatat* of an ordinary individual. The logic then follows that, as a community brings a communal bull only when there is an erroneous court ruling and a transgression made on its basis, perhaps the Anointed Priest, too, would be obliged to bring a bull in the same situation. Not so quick, as the logic might work in another way. The *chatat* brought by a Nasi as well as that brought by the Anointed Priest both differ from the *chatat* of an ordinary individual. The logic in this instance follows that, as a Nasi brings a communal bull only when there is an erroneous court ruling and a transgression made on its basis, perhaps the Anointed Priest, too, would be obliged to bring a bull in the same situation.

To whom, then, is the Anointed Priest closer for purposes of reasoning by analogy: the community or the Nasi? When it clearly violates the law, the community offers a bull; when it possibly has violated the law, though, it does not offer an *asham talui*. The Anointed Priest follows a similar pattern, and thus the analogy works between him and the community. Again, however, we need first to look back to the case of the Nasi. If the Nasi transgresses a law of idol worship, he must offer a female goat and where required a guilt offering (*asham*). The same conditions apply to the Anointed Priest, and it would appear that the analogy works between the Nasi and the Anointed Priest.

Having given logic its best shot, the Gemara retreats to repeating the scriptural verse with which it began this analysis, linking the treatment of the Anointed Priest with that of the community. All of the foregoing is part of a lengthy *baraita* that began yesterday, and before it ends it has one more question to raise. If the community must bring a bull when it transgresses the law on the basis of an erroneous court ruling, shouldn't the Anointed Priest be obliged to bring a bull when the populace similarly transgresses on the basis of his mistaken ruling? The Mishnah has it that he brings a bull only when he himself inadvertently violates the law on the basis of his own mistaken ruling. Back again to *Leviticus* 4:3, and there we learn that he and he alone brings a bull for the sins he commits.

One questionable area from the *baraita* is now brought up for analysis. It noted almost in passing that the Anointed Priest does not bring an *asham talui* (a questionable or variable guilt offering) for possible violations of the law. What would be the source for this assertion? The scriptural passage on the *asham talui* states a case of complete inadvertence, one that applies to ordinary individuals.

The Anointed Priest, being analogous to the community, brings a communal bull, not a personal *chatat*, for inadvertent commissions of transgressions that are deemed legal oversights.

Time for a new Mishnah, and this one will offer more material on the Anointed Priest. In instances in which the Anointed Priest both erroneously ruled on his own and then on the basis of his ruling acted on his own, he must make amends on his own by bringing a *chatat* bull. If he issued a mistaken ruling together with the court and then violated the law on its basis together with the community, the Anointed Priest and the community together bring a communal-error bull. The court, though, is only required to offer up a *chatat* if it repudiates part of a law and defends part of it—the same applies to the Anointed Priest. Similarly, in an instance of idol worship, the court is not obliged to offer a *chatat*—unless it repudiates part of the law and defends another part of it.

On what scriptural basis can we say that the Anointed Priest atones with a communal-error bull? Maybe he should bring a *chatat* bull on his own, when he transgresses together with the community. Logically, though, like the Nasi, if the Anointed Priest transgresses on his own, he atones with a bull on his own; so, if he transgresses with the community, he should make amends together with the community. The Gemara thus finds fault with this analogy.

The initial case of our Mishnah discusses one in which the Anointed Priest mistakenly ruled on his own and must atone on his own; the Gemara takes this to be a case in which both the Anointed Priest *and the court* (see below) offered erroneous rulings, and both he and the populace proceeded to violate the law on the basis of such a ruling. But, their separate, mistaken rulings covered different *mitzvot*. What sort of case would this involve? If the Anointed Priest is the single most brilliant sage in the Land of Israel and the court is not so well endowed, then he brings the bull to atone for himself and the court is exempt. Any person that violated the law on the basis of their ruling is obliged to bring a personal *chatat* of a female goat or lamb. If, by contrast, the court is comprised of the most brilliant minds in the Land, and the Anointed Priest is not the sharpest pin in the cushion, why would he attain atonement on his own? Shouldn't he, like the court in the previous instance, get a pass?

[a→b]

Rav Pappa attempts to save the day by claiming that this case is actually one in which both the court and the Anointed Priest were equally brilliant; this may square the circle but it does so at the expense of the symmetry of the discussion and by twisting the apparent meaning of the Mishnaic phrase.

Abaye now asks precisely what the Mishnah may have meant when it spoke of the Anointed Priest both ruling and acting "on his own" ("independently," *bifnei atsmo*). The answer would not have been clear without this exposition: It refers to a situation in which the court and the Anointed Priest issue rulings in two separate places and on two separate halachic bans. Rava suggests that they needn't be in two separate places; as long as their rulings concern "different" bans, the Anointed Priest will have acted "on his own."

Now, what precisely would have been meant by "different" halachic bans? The Gemara begins its response by ruling out the obvious. Thus, we are not speaking of the Anointed Priest allowing a forbidden fat for consumption and the court allowing something related to pagan worship—or vice versa—because these bans are clearly based on distinct scriptural verses and atonement requires different sacrificial offerings. If, though, he were to err by allowing consumption of the prohibited fat covering the innards and the court erred by allowing consumption of the prohibited fat on the intestines, we have a case in point. Are these violations of the law sufficiently distinct? Perhaps here the Anointed Priest is not atoned for with a communal bull; or, perhaps because both mention "forbidden fat" (*chelev*), this is a case of atonement through the communal bull. If the latter option is operational, what about a case in which the Anointed Priest allows consumption of forbidden fat and the court does the same for certain animal blood? Are these sufficiently distinct, or perhaps they are united by the same offering their transgression requires. No resolution: *teku*.

Toward the end of our Mishnah, the text stated that the court was only required to bring a bull *chatat* if it repudiated part of a law and defended part of it. This issue was dealt with several *dapim* ago in the discussion of an erroneous ruling covering a detail of the law, not repudiating an entire body of law. The Mishnah goes on to say that the same applies to the Anointed Priest, and we have seen how *Leviticus* 4:3 is used as a justification for this assertion.

The last phrase of our Mishnah stated that, in an instance of idol worship, the court is not obliged to offer a *chatat*—unless it repudiates part of the law and defends another part of it. We need a *baraita* to clarify things here. Idolatry is different from other transgressions, even when done inadvertently, and the required offerings are accordingly different. The *baraita* uses a *gezerah shavah* to conclude that the erroneous ruling here is that of the court and that it is for a "matter" of the law, not an entire body of it.

A new Mishnah looks at yet another comparable area in the court's and the Anointed Priest's obligations. The court is only obliged to offer a *chatat* if it errs in a matter of law and inadvertent transgression follows upon this ruling. The same applies to the Anointed Priest. Also, the court is obliged to make an offering in cases of paganism only when it errs in ruling and inadvertent transgression follows.

We basically have two rulings in this Mishnah. The source for the first one is the much used *Leviticus* 4:13 through which the Gemara concludes that, for a communal-bull obligation to become operative, both an erroneous ruling and inadvertent trangressive behavior on its basis must be present. The same conditions hold for an Anointed Priest. The second ruling in the Mishnah concerning idolatry is based on the *baraita* cited a moment ago which made use of a *gezerah shavah*. In this case, though, the Mishnah says nothing about this applying to the case of an Anointed Priest in a similar set of circumstances, implying that he would be obliged to bring a bull for an inadvertent violation.

The Gemara admits that the position stated in this Mishnah echoes the views of R. Yehudah ha-Nasi. How so? Another *baraita* teaches explicitly that R. Yehudah ha-Nasi ruled an Anointed Priest was obliged to bring a *chatat* for inadvertent violation of the law in the area of pagan worship. The sages disagree insofar as they insist that such an inadvertent act be based on a mistaken ruling concerning idolatry, though they all agree that the Anointed Priest must bring a female goat for his *chatat* for idolatry, just as would an ordinary person. They also agree that he is exempt from offering an *asham talui* in questionable cases of transgression. The Gemara has trouble with this reasoning. Relying on a Mishnah that we will cover in the next *daf*, it comes to the conclusion that the Anointed Priest is to be treated like the community, thus ultimately agreeing with the sages over R. Yehudah ha-Nasi.

Before it gives up entirely on R. Yehudah ha-Nasi's view here, though, the Gemara wants to scrutinize his logic as well as that of the sages. First, the biblical source (*Numbers* 15:28) is cited: "The priest shall provide atonement for the person who commits an inadvertence, when he transgresses inadvertently." (Alter: "And the priest shall atone for the person erring in his offense in errancy.") The term "the person" refers to the Anointed Priest, and "who commits an inadvertence" refers to the Nasi—according to the interpretation of the Gemara which can justify itself in that the phrase, "the person who commits an inadvertence," is superfluous and thus offers itself for exegesis. R. Yehudah ha-Nasi understands this to mean that the "transgression" ("sin," *chet*) spoken of here, idolatry, obliges the committer to an offering when performed inadvertently. By contrast, the rabbis see this verse meaning that the inadvertent transgressor who incurs a *chatat* obligation when he transgresses in other areas of the law also incurs a *chatat* obligation for inadvertent missteps regarding idol worship. The Anointed Priest is not covered here because, when dealing with cases other than paganism, the Anointed Priest only brings a *chatat* if he erroneously rules and then inadvertently acts on his erroneous ruling.

The *baraita* went on to state that R. Yehudah ha-Nasi and the sages do agree that in cases involving idol worship the Anointed Priest must bring a female goat, just as would an individual. The scriptural source here (*Numbers* 15:27) speaks of an "individual" (*nefesh*; Alter: "single person") transgressing the law inadvertently, making no distinction as to whether such an individual is an ordinary person, the Anointed Priest, or even the Nasi. The Gemara will pick up this theme on the following *daf*.

HORAYOT 8

Our new *daf* begins with the tail end of an explanation of a lengthy *baraita*. This final piece concerns the ruling that an Anointed Priest does not offer up an *asham talui*. Inasmuch as the pertinent verse here (*Leviticus* 5:18) speaks of the commission of an inadvertent act as that which leads to an *asham talui*, the Gemara interprets (perhaps, overinterprets) this as *solely* an inadvertent act but not one also brought on by a mistaken ruling as well. The latter is required for an Anointed Priest to be obliged in an *asham talui*. An instance of idol worship would seem to be an exception here, but R. Yehudah ha-Nasi interprets it in the same way. Actually, we learn that R. Yehudah ha-Nasi explains that only in a case of pagan worship would the Anointed Priest need bring a *chatat* for an inadvertence alone, but in instances involving all the other *mitzvot* of the Torah, he must both issue an erroneous ruling and then inadvertently transgress on its basis. The rabbis read the verse in question to exempt the Anointed Priest from an *asham talui* even in cases of possible pagan worship; in no instance, including idol worship, is he obliged to offer a *chatat* for an inadvertent act alone, they claim.

A new Mishnah now discusses differences in this same theme between the court and the Anointed Priest. (The text neatly parallels other Mishnayot that have preceded it.) When must the court bring a communal-error bull? Only when it rules mistakenly on a prohibition whose deliberate transgression would result in excision (*karet*) and whose unintentional transgression obliges it to bring a *chatat*. Ditto for the Anointed Priest. When does the court incur a *chatat* for pagan worship? Only when it mistakenly rules on an issue involving idolatry whose deliberate transgression would result in excision and whose unintentional transgression obliges it to bring a *chatat*.

The Gemara begins by seeking a scriptural source for the first case. R. Yehudah ha-Nasi constructs a *gezerah shavah* by linking the passage dealing with communal bulls (*Leviticus* 4:14) and another passage (*Leviticus* 4:18) prohibiting a man from marrying his wife's sister while she (his wife) is alive. Both verses use the term *aleha* ("upon which," "upon her"), the basis for the *gezerah* shavah, and in both cases the punishment for a deliberate transgression is excision and the punishment for unintentional transgression is a *chatat*. (It is a little difficult to imagine a case of unintentionally marrying one's wife's sister, but let's leave that particular difficulty to another tractate. Perhaps, if one is led to the *chupah* without as yet seeing one's second [or third] "intended," one might discover such a transgression after the exchange of vows and the Seven Blessings have been enunciated and upon removing her veil.) What about the Anointed Priest in such an instance? First, the oft-used verse in *Leviticus* 4:3 equates, if properly interpreted, the conditions for a community's liability in a *chatat* with that of the Anointed Priest. Then, the Gemara resorts to another *gezerah shavah* linking a passage about the Nasi with a passage about the community concerning violation of "one of all the commandments." In both cases deliberate transgression leads to excision, and unintentional transgression to a *chatat*. And, while we're at it, the Gemara adds that the same applies to an ordinary individual. It explains that because a passage about the individual transgressing the law follows directly on the heels of the passage about the Nasi and because it begins with the connective "and," the two passages are linked and the teachings about the Nasi apply as well to an ordinary individual.

Moving right along to the next portion of the Mishnah, the Gemara wants to know the scriptural source for obliging a court to bring a *chatat* in cases involving idol worship only when it issues a mistaken ruling which leads to transgressive actions by the community which, if done purposefully, would lead to excision. The rabbis here point out that the Bible distinguishes communal pagan worship from all other transgressions, discussing the two in separate places. One might, thus, think that they need be dealt with in entirely different ways. However, the rabbis use another *gezerah shavah* to link the two and come to the conclusion as presented in the Mishnah. Ordinary individuals are added to the list (along with the Nasi and the Anointed Priest) of those obliged to a *chatat* for accidental pagan worship by virtue of the same connective "and," albeit in a different place in the Bible.

The Gemara above used the dual appearances of the term *aleha* to establish a *gezerah shavah* and make its case. That was reasoning marshaled by R. Yehudah ha-Nasi. The rabbis, however, use the same *gezerah shavah* of *aleha* for another ruling altogether, meaning that it is not available for them to make the case about deliberate transgression vs. unintentional transgression where the former causes excision and the latter must lead to a *chatat*. What source or sources do they use to make that case?

They cite a teaching of R. Yehoshua ben Levi. *Numbers* (15:29-31) contains several crucial passages in this regard. First, it speaks of an individual who "inadvertently" transgresses any law of the

Torah; then, it immediately segues to an individual who behaves "high-handedly" and shows contempt for the "word of God," an implication of engaging in pagan worship. These two passages are linked by the slightly earlier biblical passage (15:27) on *chatat* obligation, thus analogizing idol worship with the other prohibitions of the Torah. Hence, as with other deliberate violations, so too with deliberate acts of pagan worship, where excision is the rule, with unintentional transgression a *chatat* obligation ensues. The rabbis' reasoning concludes with a logical inference making the same argument for the ordinary individual who commits such sins.

How would R. Yehudah ha-Nasi deal with the verse (*Numbers* 15:29: "There shall be a single law for you, for one who acts inadvertently"; Alter: "one teaching there shall be for them for him who does in errancy") used for this exegesis by the rabbis? He uses this law to make the point that, in matters of inadvertent violation of the law prohibiting pagan worship, there are no distinctions between the individual and the masses. By contrast, in matters of deliberate violation there are. And, as for the *chatat* that must be brought, everyone involved in a communal violation of the law prohibiting idolatry brings the same standard one for individuals.

The Gemara to this Mishnah concludes with a roundabout discussion of several biblical passages we have been using from *Numbers* and *Leviticus*. The effort is to ascertain which violations are being referred to for special sacrificial offerings. The text goes to great lengths to prove that the prime commandment, the one that equals all the others combined, the first one sent by God to the Jewish people either directly or via Moses, the very first one was against idolatry, which must be it. It marshals a lot of evidence, but ends by saying no—and then abruptly segues to a new Mishnah, leaving things a bit confused.

[a→b]

The new Mishnah follows on the previous one by examining relevant situations in which such rulings would apply. For example, the court need not bring a communal-error bull for violations of all commandments, positive and negative, concerning pollution of the Temple. Similarly, an ordinary individual need not offer up an *asham talui* for possible violations of any of the commandments concerning polluting the Temple. Violation on the part of the court of any commandment, positive or negative, concerning a *niddah*, though, does result in a communal-bull obligation. Similarly, possible violations by an individual of any commandment concerning a *niddah* results in an *asham talui*. The Mishnah ends with two rhetorical questions to clarify that the positive commandment concerning a *niddah* is to stay away from a *niddah*, and the negative commandment is not to have relations with a *niddah*. These appear to be two sides of the same coin.

The Gemara starts by asking for a source for the first declaration of the Mishnah about the court's exemption from a communal bull. This leads to some seriously circuitous "reasoning" about the types of transgressions for which fixed *chatat* offerings are required and from there arguing back to the *asham talui*, using a complex *gezerah shavah*. The Gemara itself rejects this reasoning by finding another instance of the use of the same term used in the *gezerah shavah* which offers a better option. Some more wrangling about the nature of words used in a *gezerah shavah*—namely, words with the same root though in different forms, and even synonyms, are potentially acceptable. The Gemara restates its derivation again, is rebutted by one or another authority, and then restates it once more. The argumentation here, I must admit, is so arcane as to almost make one forget where it began. It is this sort of difficulty for which the Talmud is justifiably famous, setting its bar to comprehension so high that it defeats many who have attempted to penetrate it.

The next Mishnah begins with a ruling from R. Yose Haglili that a court—and the Nasi—is exempt from bringing an offering in cases of "hearing a voice of adjuration" (lying under oath) or polluting the Temple or its holies (cases in which an individual would be obliged in a variable *chatat*, variable due to the financial state of its bearer). R. Akiva disagrees and claims that the Nasi does become liable for violations in the latter two of these instances. He is not liable for "hearing a voice of adjuration," because the ruler is legally bound neither to judge nor to be judged, nor may he testify or be testified against (a view based on *Deuteronomy* 17:15). There is thus both a separate judiciary and a ruler above or outside the law.

The Gemara begins with Ulla asking what R. Yose Haglili's source would have been for ruling the Nasi not liable for a variable *chatat* in these instances. R. Yose Haglili, we are told, interprets a verse (*Leviticus* 5:5) to mean that anyone who can conceivably be obliged to make an offering in these cases does, indeed, become obliged when he commits such a transgression. By the same token, whoever can't be obliged isn't. The Gemara objects that the same reasoning could be turned on its head. So, it tries again and suggests that R. Yose Haglili's justification emerges from a *baraita*, but before the *baraita* can even get off the ground, our *daf* comes to an abrupt end. We'll pick it up on the next *daf*.

HORAYOT 9

The previous *daf* ended as R. Yose Haglili's reasoning was being unpacked with a *baraita* in which R. Yirmyah was explaining that a variable *chatat* is incurred for someone whose financial situation has changed, either from wealth to poverty or vice versa, but never for the Nasi or the Anointed Priest because they will always, of course, be wealthy. By way of explanation, there are three levels of wealth articulated: a rich man offers a sheep or goat, a poorer man of more modest means offers two turtledoves or young doves, and a poor person offers one-tenth of an *efah* (equal to 3 *seot*, or 18 *kabim*, or 72 *lugin*, or a volume of 432 eggs, roughly) of fine flour;

and the transgressions requiring a variable *chatat* are polluting the Temple and lying in court under oath. One can already see the challenges coming, but before we get there the Gemara cites a handful of passages from the Torah and the Mishnah to support the idea that the holders of these two posts can ever descend into poverty. That is, because neither can ever be less than wealthy, they are not subject to the variable *chatat*. (This doesn't mean they are exempt for these particular violations of the law, but only that the prescribed offerings linked to the variable *chatat* are not applicable here.)

Now come the challenges. Ravina asks about the case of a Nasi who comes down with *tzara'at*, that skin disease often mistranslated as leprosy, because he must abdicate in such a case. Is he then no longer considered royalty and subject to this law, or does he always remain immune to a variable *chatat*? Rav Nachman bar Yitzchak answers that, *tzara'at* or no *tzara'at*, he's still extraordinarily rich and not ever going to fall into genuine poverty.

In the case of the Anointed Priest, we hear from R. Akiva in a *baraita* that he is free from obligation to a variable *chatat* for commission of all three of the transgressions which oblige it. Rava offers some explanation, via *Leviticus* 6:13, for why the Anointed Priest would not be required ever to bring a one-tenth *efah* of flour. But that still leaves the other two levels of wealth. The discussion then begins to spin out of control about who is liable for what. Does "one of these" equal or imply "each and every one," the text asks. After much wrangling and fancy footwork, the Gemara concludes that, just as the Anointed Priest is exempt from a poor person's offering ("one of these"), he is similarly exempt from the others' as well ("each and every one").

If there was ever a time for a new Mishnah, this is probably it. We move to a discussion in this one to three kinds of offerings for transgressions. It starts with the *chatat*. For any *mitzvah* whose deliberate transgression would incur excision, unintentional violation obliges one to bring a *chatat*: for ordinary individuals, a female lamb or goat; for the Nasi, a male goat; and for the Anointed Priest or court, a bull. If the unintentional violation was a case of idol worship, the *chatat* is: a female goat for an ordinary individual, the Nasi, or the Anointed Priest; a bull and male goat for the court, with the bull as an *olah* (or burnt offering) and the goat as a *chatat*. Much of this we have been introduced to *en passant* earlier.

The Mishnah moves on to present the *asham* offerings. An ordinary individual and the Nasi are obliged to bring an *asham talui* (the questionable guilt offering) for the inadvertent possible transgression of a ban for whose deliberate commission one would incur excision, but the Anointed Priest and the court are exempt. The definite *asham* is incumbent upon an ordinary individual, the Nasi, and the Anointed Priest, but the court remains exempt. Again, some of this we have already confronted in passing.

Finally, it takes up the variable *chatat* which one incurs for "hearing a voice of adjuration," making a false oath (lying about a past event or swearing to do something in future and then breaking that promise), or polluting the Temple or its holies. According to R. Shimon, the court is exempt, but an ordinary individual, the Nasi, and the Anointed Priest are all possible candidates. The Anointed Priest, though, is exempt from the last transgression, polluting the Temple. R. Eliezer further explains that the variable *chatat* offering required of the Nasi is a male goat, the same as his offering for a fixed *chatat*.

The Gemara (from whom I for one am hoping for a lot of help) begins with a *baraita* that offers R. Shimon's overview of the groupings for liability: (1) For whatever an ordinary individual may incur an *asham talui*, the Nasi is also obliged, but the Anointed Priest and the court are not; (2) for whatever an ordinary individual may incur a definite *asham*, both the Nasi and the Anointed Priest are also obliged, but the court is not; (3) for the three transgressions of "hearing a voice of adjuration," making a false oath, or polluting the Temple or its holies, the Nasi and the Anointed Priest are obliged to offer a variable *chatat*—just like an ordinary individual—save the Nasi is exempt for the transgression of "hearing a voice of adjuration" and the Anointed Priest is exempt for polluting the Temple or its holies; and (4) whenever an ordinary individual must bring a variable *chatat*, so too is the Nasi, but the court and the Anointed Priest are not.

Thankfully, the Gemara immediately jumps on what appears to be a blatant contradiction. The Anointed Priest is listed initially as exempt from a variable *chatat* for polluting the Temple or its holies, clearly implying obligations on his part for violating the other two sins in this list of three. The end of the *baraita* giving R. Shimon's overview claims that whenever an ordinary individual must bring a variable *chatat*, so too must the Nasi, but the court and the Anointed Priest are not exempt. If the court and the Anointed Priest are equal in this regard, then whenever the court is not liable, the Anointed Priest should also not be liable.

[a→b]

Rav Huna son of Rav Yehoshua "resolves" the apparent contradiction by claiming that the initial implication that the Anointed Priest may sometimes be liable to a variable *chatat* concerns the modest or wealthy form of the offering, whereas the latter reference is to the poor man's offering (of fine flour). While R. Akiva exempts the Anointed Priest from all three levels of variable *chatat*, R. Shimon agrees that the Anointed Priest is exempt from the poor man's offering, but only that and not the other two levels.

Chizkiyah offers a scriptural support for R. Shimon's statement that the Anointed Priest is exempt for polluting the Temple or its holies. The reasoning employed involves differences in the items offered, and the Gemara raises a number of potential difficulties that might involve other groups as potential exemptees as well. Rava steps in and saves the day by rewording R. Shimon's views.

The Mishnah ended with a statement from R. Eliezer explaining that the variable *chatat* offering required of the Nasi is a male goat for polluting the Temple or its holies. By way of further explanation, R. Yochanan notes that in so doing the Nasi is bringing the same offering as he would for a fixed *chatat*, and this makes sense in context. In an uncommon show of unity, Rav Pappa agrees as well and adds an explanation for why this offering required of the Nasi applies solely for this violation (and not the others) and why the Anointed Priest is exempt for this one as well. Rav Huna son of Rav Natan contests Rav Pappa, but the latter effectively rebuts the former's arguments and concludes: "And, there is nothing more" to say on this matter, usually indicating that there may, indeed, be more, even much more, but I don't think we need to go there.

One more piece of fine-tuning on R. Yochanan's part: By stating his ruling in the manner in which he did, R. Eliezer implies that the Nasi does not bring an *asham talui*. As our chapter is winding down, a professional reciter of *baraitot* (an occupation recalling a time before these texts were written down and, of course, well before the invention and spread of print) announces in the presence of Rav Sheshet that an *asham talui* is incurred for possible pollution of the Temple or its holies. Rav Sheshet rejects this assertion or at least the way it is phrased, and he cites R. Yochanan's citation of R. Eliezer to the effect that the Nasi is not liable for an *asham talui*. Ultimately, the Gemara leaves this one unresolved—the *baraita* jibes with no known Tanna's views on the matter, meaning that the *baraita* may not be authoritative, an interesting conclusion from the perspective of Talmudic exegeses.

Chapter Three

An Anointed Priest Sinned
(*dapim* 9b-14a)

HORAYOT 9B (CONTINUED)

Always interested in saving paper, our green antecedents of pre-modern times squeezed the very beginning of the next and final chapter of this tractate onto the bottom of this *daf*. The first Mishnah carries on the theme of laws involving the special offerings incurred by the Anointed Priest and the ruler. This Mishnah also takes up what I would see as a problem unaddressed in a previous Mishnah on our *daf*: What happens when the social (or economic) station of a sinner changes? In a case when the Anointed Priest or the Nasi committed a transgression of the law and then left office, the former brings a bull as his *chatat*, while the latter offers a male goat. In both instances, it is the station of the sinner at the time of the violation that determines the offering incurred. If an Anointed Priest or the Nasi left office and then committed a transgression of the law, the former brings a bull as his *chatat*, but the Nasi is no different now from an ordinary person and thus his offering is the same, a female goat or lamb.

The Gemara gets only five words before breaking off for a new *daf*, not even a full sentence.

HORAYOT 10

In both instances recorded in the Mishnah here, the Anointed Priest faces the same required offering. Why were both rulings, sinning before and after leaving office, issued? The former—before stepping down—is fairly obvious, but the Gemara essentially claims that both halves of the overall ruling had to be enunciated for stylistic reasons, an interesting point. Then, there is the matter of the latter ruling—namely, that even after leaving office first and then violating the law, a former Anointed Priest is still obliged to bring a bull. In explaining this ruling, the Gemara cites a *baraita* for its source. The frequently cited verse *Leviticus* 4:3 states clearly that the Anointed Priest brings his special *chatat* of a bull, and it makes no mention of before or after. Logic—which must be taken somewhat on trust (something of an oxymoron, I realize) because it is convoluted, to say the least—might dictate otherwise, but this verse trumps logic here. The Nasi's situation is somewhat different, for the verse used to substantiate the requirement of his special *chatat* (*Leviticus* 4:22) stipulates a ruler (*Nasi*) transgressing, and thus once he has stepped down or abdicated, he is no longer considered a ruler, just a commoner—and thus requiring a different offering.

Quickly on to another Mishnah, and this one concerns the other end of the spectrum—offerings incurred by the Anointed Priest and the Nasi before they ascend to their exalted posts. In such an instance of violation of the law followed by elevation to one of these positions, both are treated as ordinary commoners. R. Shimon adds a ripple: If they became aware of their transgression before taking office, they bring a commoner's *chatat*, but if they become aware of their transgression after acceding to high office, they are not liable. In his view, awareness of a transgression is just as important as commission of it. The Mishnah next asks who is referred to in the verses under examination (*Leviticus* 4:22-26) when the term "*Nasi*" is used and a special *chatat* outlined. Answer: The king, the man at the pinnacle of political power. The explanation for this derivation will appear on the following *daf*, and we shall deal with it there.

The Gemara begins where it frequently does, by citing a *baraita* which asks what the scriptural source would be for the first ruling of the Mishnah about considering the Nasi and Anointed Priest who violated the law prior to elevation as if they were commoners. *Leviticus* 4:3 (again) speaks of the Anointed Priest possibly sinning in the future, which is interpreted to mean that the violation occurred prior to taking office. As we saw a moment ago, one might think that logic would dictate such a conclusion—implying, interestingly, the lack of a need for a scriptural source upon which to base such a judgment. Bottom line is that the status of he who would be an Anointed Priest at the time of the commission of the transgression is crucial. If he has not yet risen to this high post, he is effectively a commoner; once he is the Anointed Priest, he perforce is obliged to bring his special *chatat*.

The Gemara then proceeds in parallel fashion to cite a *baraita* for the ruling about the Nasi. *Leviticus* 4:22 would seem to parallel for the Nasi what 4:3 did for the Anointed Priest, distinguishing before and after the commission of a transgression. Again, we are intriguingly asked if we could have gone straight to a logical explanation of this ruling without any need for a scriptural source. And, once again, the Gemara rejects this avenue in favor of the verse which it interprets to mean: When the Nasi commits a sin while in office, he is obliged to offer the special *chatat* designated under the law; when he is not yet the Nasi, he is just like everyone else (except maybe the Anointed Priest).

The Gemara next introduces another fascinating *baraita* to clarify the parallelism between the two verses cited with respect to the commission of a transgression by the Anointed Priest and the Nasi. In *Leviticus* 4:22, the phrase translated as "when a Nasi will sin" (*asher Nasi yecheta*; Alter: "When a chieftain offends") might imply that it is foredoomed that the Nasi will indeed violate the law, but the *baraita* snuffs out such an assumption by lining up our parallelism and stating that this *asher* is comparable to the *im* (if) in the phrase "if the Anointed Priest will sin" (*im hakohen hamashiach yecheta*) and thus means "if" or, more precisely, "when." Does the Torah ever decree that the Nasi will sin? Rather than calm our collective nerves, the sages respond that, yes, it does and several rabbis offer their views. The conclusion to this string is that the use of *im* (lit., "if") in this context with *yecheta* ("he will sin") must mean "if" and does not mean a definite sin will ensue (as the use of "when" might imply). Grammar can be extremely important.

The Gemara now spins off into a digression suggested by R. Shimon that concerns *tzara'at*. Rather than follow it, let us move to the next section which takes a closer look at the phrase "when a Nasi will sin" and proposes that this would exclude an ill Nasi from his obligation to bring a special *chatat*. Does illness really spell expulsion from office? As Rav Avdimi bar Chama attempts to clarify, "illness" here refers to a Nasi who has come down with *tzara'at*, and in this case the Nasi is considered as a ruler who has stepped down. A verse from *II Kings* (15:5) supports this line of reasoning.

To illustrate this lesson the Gemara recounts a long anecdote between Rabban Gamliel and R. Yehoshua. How it ties up with our Gemara and in fact "illustrates" the case at hand is extremely difficult to see, but the story is interesting in and of itself.

[a→b]

The Gemara moves along to take yet another look at the verse "when (*asher*) a Nasi will sin." In its fuller form, the verse speaks of an unintentional transgression and the offering the Nasi brings. Because of a similarity in language, Rabban Yochanan ben Zakkai declares it "fortunate" (*ashrei*) to have a ruler who brings a *chatat*, and he will be an inspiration to ordinary folk. Rava son of Rabbah disagrees with such an exegesis because it might mean associating every instance of *asher* with *ashrei*, and he proceeds to cite a few in which "fortunate" would definitely not apply as a proper translation or, at least, lexical association. The Gemara responds that such was not Rabban Yochanan ben Zakkai's intention; he says the biblical text had a purposeful intent in inserting the word *asher* here, breaking with the grammar used nearby and thus calling for exegesis.

The Gemara doesn't contest this answer and in fact offers another instance in *Kohelet* (8:14). Rav Nachman bar Rav Chisda cites the verse here in which the word *asher* might be understood as *ashrei* (meaning "fortunate"). In sum, the text compares the way the righteous are mistreated in this world with the (presumed) suffering of the wicked in the next, just as the wicked enjoy this world and the righteous will have a blissful eternity in the next. Rava doesn't buy such a reading, asking the obvious but telling question: Can't the righteous enjoy their lives in both realms? He would have us understand the scriptural phrase as wishing the righteous to enjoy this world just as the wicked do, and woe betide the day the wicked are forced to face the music in this world as the righteous ordinarily face hardship in same. To buttress this case, the Gemara tells of two Torah scholars (Rav Pappa and Rav Huna son of Rav Yehoshua) who were asked by Rava if they had learned certain tractates well, and they replied that they had; he then asked them if they had acquired a modest amount of wealth, and they assured him that they each had small pieces of land which provided for them nicely. Moral: You can be a righteous person and find happiness, or at least satisfaction, in this world.

Still on a bit of a digression comparing the fates of wicked and righteous persons, the Gemara looks at how they compare when doing the same thing. Rabbah bar Bar Chanah cites a passage from *Hosea* (14:10) about how the righteous walk the straight and narrow path set by God while the wicked trip and fall. Example: Two men cook their Passover offerings, but one does it to fulfill the *mitzvah*, while the other does it to wolf down the tasty meat. The former corresponds to the righteous man in the verse, the latter to the wicked man.

Resh Lakish doesn't appreciate the exegesis. How can we characterize the latter—the glutton who ate for the pure pleasure of it—as wicked? Whatever his aim, he did at least fulfill the *mitzvah*. No, he argues, a better comparison with the verse would be two married men, both of whom have their wives and a sister with them at home. Both wish to engage in conjugal relations with their spouse. One happens upon his wife and proceeds, while the other happens upon her sister and proceeds. The former is the righteous man in the verse, the latter the wicked one. But, the verse spoke of a single road, and Resh Lakish effectively posits two.

One more comparative example, which leads to a lengthy digression: the (in)famous case of Lot and his daughters. The only survivors of the annihilation of Sodom and Gomorrah, the daughters feared the whole world had been destroyed and thought their father was the last man alive on earth. To save the human race, they realized they would have to cohabit with their own father. So, they got him drunk and his older daughter slept with her own father, became pregnant, and ultimately gave birth to a son named Moab; the next night his younger daughter did the same with the same result, producing a son named Ben Ami. The daughters aimed to fulfill a *mitzvah*, though Lot exemplified the wicked sinner. Wait, though, for Lot, too, may have intended to fulfill the same *mitzvah*. R. Yochanan argues against such a notion, as he sees Lot as a pathological sinner; he cites *Genesis* 13:10 about Lot's decision to settle in Sodom which looks unobjectionable on the surface, but which he finds through various means to be immoral through and through. Maybe it was beyond Lot's capacity to think rationally, given how inebriated he was at the time of his cohabitation with his daughters. The Gemara employs a subtle—indeed so subtle it's almost impossible to see—explicatory technique to try to refute this line. Last try: Maybe Lot was so far gone that before he knew what had happened, the transgression was already done. Well, the Gemara interestingly suggests that, if he really regretted his sin when he got up the next day, then he should not have allowed his younger daughter to ply him with wine the next night and repeat the entire mess, which he did.

One digression leads to another. Rabbah asks for the meaning of *Proverbs* 18:19, and he explains that it is a (highly cloaked) reference to Lot. Then, Rava does the same with *Proverbs* 18:1. One consequence of Lot's actions is that descendants of Moab (Moabites) and Ben Ami (Ammonites) may never marry into the Jewish people.

Ulla offers another comparative case of sinning for different aims with different results. Tamar and Zimri both had sexual relations with forbidden partners, Tamar with Judah, the father of her late husband, and Zimri (head of the tribe of Shimon) with Cozbi, a Moabite princess. Because her aims were dignified and righteous, Tamar spawned (ultimately) the Davidic dynasty; because Zimri's aims were base, however, thousands of Israelites died as a result.

Still on the theme of sinful behavior with righteous aims, Rav Nachman bar Yitzchak claims that it is better to violate the law for the sake of Heaven than to do a *mitzvah* for base or self-serving ends. He offers an example, but the Gemara immediately questions the principle. It cites a view of Rav, articulated by Rav Yehudah, that one should always study Torah and do *mitzvot* even for dubious ends. The reason is that, ultimately, Torah study and the performance of *mitzvot* will lead a person to higher moral ground and to doing the same for Heaven's sake. That leads the Gemara to rephrase Rav Nachman bar Yitzchak's principle to equate sinning for the sake of Heaven with carrying out *mitzvot* for questionable ends. The Gemara takes apart, in lurid detail, the putative sin raised by Rav Nachman bar Yitzchak and wonders why the woman involved, Yael, seemed to enjoy her sinning so much. It rebuts this insinuation and then moves back into the realm of principle. What proof do we have to substantiate Rav's view about Torah study and performing *mitzvot*? Citation from *Numbers* 23 and the alleged forty-two sacrifices of the evil Balak follow. What good was the result? Ruth descended from him, and generations later King David. The subject of Torah study and *mitzvah* performance not for their own sake is a major theme running through a number of Talmudic tractates, especially *Bereshit*.

Back briefly to the story of Lot and his two daughters, as our *daf* winds down, generations later Moses would not allow the children of Israel to go into battle against the Moabites. Perhaps more on this on the next *daf*.

HORAYOT 11

So, Moses forbid the children of Israel from all-out battle against the Moabites, though he did allow for badgering them. The Gemara suggests (homiletically, to be sure) that this is because the name this older daughter of Lot chose for her son, Moab (lit., from Father), broadcast the illicit nature of the union that produced him. By contrast, her sister chose the more modest name of Ben Ami (lit., son of my people) for her illicit child, and God forbade Moses from fighting with Ben Ami's descendants in any fashion whatsoever. The Gemara also notes another moral from the story of Lot's daughters: always seek to perform a *mitzvah* first. The older daughter was rewarded (so to speak) for becoming impregnated by her father first by having her descendants attain royal standing four generations before her younger sister.

Back to our Mishnah and to a *baraita* elucidating its laws regarding individual *chataot*. The latter are to be brought by individuals "from among the people of the land" after an inadvertent violation. The quoted passage would rule out both the Anointed Priest and the Nasi, as neither is an ordinary individual. Then, the Gemara questions the necessity of this derivation when the text already explicitly distinguished them with special offerings. As we have seen earlier, the thrust of the argument demanding the *baraita*'s derivation is that the Anointed Priest and the Nasi are both exempt from any *chatat* obligation if they transgress by inadvertence alone (meaning without an oversight on their part beforehand).

The Gemara accepts this argument as far as the Anointed Priest is concerned, but what about the Nasi who has a special male goat obligation for an inadvertent sin alone. What, then, would have been the purpose of the additional verse stating that he is exempt from bringing a commoner's offering? Rav Zevid comes up with a rather far-fetched answer, which will be immediately disputed. He claims that the case at hand is one in which the Nasi-elect eats an olive-sized (*kezayit*) piece of forbidden animal fat (*chelev*), the required amount to constitute a bona fide transgression, then becomes Nasi, and only then becomes aware of his sin. Because he was an ordinary commoner at the time of the transgression, one might think he would be obliged to bring the offering required for such, but the phrase "from the people of the land" leads us away from such a conclusion.

This line of reasoning follows that of R. Shimon who holds that the moment of awareness of a transgression is critical to assessing the appropriate offering. However, the rabbis look only at the moment when the transgression took place, and they thus dispute Rav Zevid's exegesis. Maybe, suggests the Gemara, Rav Zevid argued somewhat differently. Maybe, the Nasi-elect ate one-half of an olive's volume of forbidden fat, was then elevated to Nasi, and only then ate the other half. It was only at that point that his transgression came to his attention. Lest one think the two halves here combine to constitute a transgression necessitating a commoner's offering, the phrase "from the people of the land" (somehow) teaches that he is exempt altogether.

Rava was similarly interested in how being in the position of Nasi might constitute a separation with regard to *chatat* obligations.

Thus, what would happen if a man ate half an olive-volume of forbidden fat, then became the Nasi, then stepped down from the rulership, and only then ate the other half olive-volume of the fat? In the previous case, as explained by Rav Zevid, are we to understand that the two halves don't make a whole because he ate half while a commoner and half after becoming the Nasi? In this case, then, do the two halves make a whole, halachically speaking, inasmuch as he consumed the two halves while in the station of a commoner (interrupted only by his rise and decline as Nasi)? Perhaps the fact that he rose to serving as the Nasi in between consumption of the two halves forms a separation and prevents a combination from taking place.

One possible solution is offered by Ulla channeling R. Yochanan. A man accidentally eats some forbidden fat, becomes aware of his transgression, and sets aside a *chatat* offering. Then, though, he abandons Judaism altogether, only later to return to the faith of his fathers and mothers. The *chatat* that he abandoned remains unacceptable to the Altar. Ulla and R. Yochanan see this as similar to our case in that service as the Nasi causes him to have "abandoned" a commoner's *chatat*. But, the Gemara finds this analogy bogus. An apostate has no right to bring an offering, while a Nasi sure does. Whatever offering the apostate set aside before abandoning his faith is forever abandoned, even when he returns to the faith.

Another related case is suggested when R. Zera asks Rav Sheshet the following. Suppose the Nasi, before assuming that post, ate some fat whose status was in doubt and he was unaware of it. Then, he was elevated to become the Nasi and only then did this doubt become known to him. Must he bring an *asham talui*? The rabbis who take the time of the transgression as crucial answer: yes, of course, because when he committed the violation he was a commoner, and commoners are obliged to bring an *asham talui* under such circumstances. R. Shimon, who takes both time of commission and moment of awareness of the transgression into account, might think that, because his change in status when rising to the throne would lead to an exemption for a known violation, perhaps it would exempt him for an *asham talui* due to an unclear violation. The Gemara then argues the exact opposite conclusion based on R. Shimon's approach. Ultimately, no answer is forthcoming: *teku*.

Back to the phrase "from the people of the land" which a *baraita* teaches as applicable to any Jew who transgresses inadvertently, except for a renegade or apostate. How do we know this? *Leviticus* 4:22-23 holds someone who would ordinarily not transgress (if he knew better) responsible for a *chatat* for an inadvertent act. Someone whose knowledge would not inhibit their transgressive behavior brings no *chatat* for an inadvertent act. Rav Hamnuna offers one explanation of this case, but it is promptly rejected out of hand.

There appears to be some question as to what constitutes a renegade here. The case may be one of a man who consumes *nevelah* (unslaughtered and hence unkosher meat) because he likes the taste (he'd eat kosher meat if given an opportunity, but he consumes non-kosher meat and forbidden fat) as well as forbidden fat that he thought was allowable. When he became aware of his actions, he wanted to bring the requisite *chatat*. One authority tells him to forget it, because he is a renegade by virtue of his willingness to consume *nevelah* purely for self-gratification. R. Shimon, though, absolves him of renegade status because of his desire to eat kosher, were it available to him; he thus may bring his *chatat*.

A *baraita* connected to this string is now cited to the effect that one who consumes the forbidden fat of a ritually slaughtered animal is a renegade. Then, it asks the question: What is a renegade? And, gets a different answer: One who consumes *nevelot, terefot* (animals with one of a number of specified physical problems which doom the animal), vile and disgusting creatures, or *nesech* (pagan libational) wine. R. Yehudah would add someone who wears *kilayim* (garments with mixed wool and linen, also known as *sha'atnez*) to the list. The Gemara then asks the question all readers must have mentally posed: What in the world is going on here? First, the *baraita* defines a renegade, and then it redefines the term differently. Rabbah bar Bar Chanah tries out an explanation. Consuming forbidden fat because one enjoys the taste does make one a renegade, but consuming it out of pure rebelliousness vis-à-vis the Torah qualifies one as a Sadducee. And, the typical Sadducee renegade is one who consumes *nevelot, terefot,* vile and disgusting creatures, or *nesech* wine.

Apparently following his father's tradition, R. Yose son of R. Yehudah adds that wearing *kilayim* is something renegades as a rule do. The difference between these views is that the addition of wearing *kilayim* is rabbinic in nature, whereas the original author of the *baraita* required biblical prohibitions to constitute the behavior of a renegade. R. Yose son of R. Yehudah would define a *kilayim* wearer in that renegade category, thus accepting rabbinic rulings as well.

The definitional issue of renegade vs. Sadducee is next posed for further clarification. Rav Acha and Ravina apparently disagreed on this topic, and although the Gemara lays out two divergent points of view, it doesn't tell us who adopted which. One defines anyone who consumes forbidden fat and *nevelot* for the love of their taste as a renegade; if he does it to rebel against the Torah, he is defined as a Sadducee. The other defines this rebelliousness as constitutive of a renegade's behavior; a Sadducee is defined as one who bows down to idols. The first of these constructions of a Sadducee seems to contradict a *baraita* which teaches that anyone who would eat a flea or a gnat is a renegade (in addition to being marginally insane, one might add). This behavior would have to be in rebelliousness against the Torah, because there is clearly no desire to savor the flavor of such bugs; nonetheless, the *baraita* deems him a renegade, not a Sadducee. The response is that the person involved claimed that he explicitly wanted to taste a forbidden item; hence, he consumed the disgusting bug not directly as a rebellious act against the Torah but out of a (perverse) desire for an outlawed "food" item. He might thus be deemed a Sadducee.

Back to the Mishnah's definition of the Nasi as the king (*melech*) and the question of what to do when he violates the law.

[a→b]

The Gemara clarifies through a *gezerah shavah* that the term Nasi is being used here as the ruler above all the people and having only God above him, and not in the sense of "prince" of one of the tribes, who would be subservient to the king.

Along similar lines, R. Yehudah ha-Nasi as the leader of the Jewish people in the Land of Israel asked R. Chiyya, if he (R. Yehudah ha-Nasi) were to inadvertently transgress (and the Temple were still standing), would he bring a male goat like the Nasi. R. Chiyya, in so many words, states that his interlocutor (and teacher) was subservient to the Resh Galuta (leader of the Diaspora, descendant of the Davidic dynasty) in Babylonia; his *chatat* would thus be no different from that of a commoner. R. Yehudah ha-Nasi responds that there was a time when two regimes ruled in the Land, and the kings of each would, upon commission of an inadvertent transgression, bring a *chatat* independently. R. Chiyya replies that those two kings were of equal standing, neither superior to the other, but you (my teacher and friend) are a status level beneath the Resh Galuta.

As often happens, the Gemara now retells the same story, with a slightly different twist. Here is Rav Safra's version. When R. Yehudah ha-Nasi asked his initial question, R. Chiyya gave a different answer: The leader in Babylonia is called a "scepter" (a rod) and the leader in Israel is known as a "legislator" (a scholar). A *baraita* supports this by asserting that the scepter rules, and the legislator teaches Torah in public. This is the long answer for why R. Yehudah ha-Nasi does not bring the *chatat* of a Nasi.

Time for a new Mishnah, this one centering on a definition of the Anointed Priest. In answer to this definitional question, the

Mishnah states that it is the High Priest (Kohen gadol) anointed with the special anointing oil, not the High Priest with the additional vestments (and no anointing oil). The only difference between these two kinds of High Priest is that only the anointed one brings a bull for erroneous rulings. The only difference between an attending High Priest and one who substitutes for the attending High Priest when he must step aside because he has become impure or in any other way unfit for service is the Yom Kippur bull and the daily one-tenth *efah* of flour, special offerings brought only by the attending High Priest. The rest of the Yom Kippur services may be handled by either High Priest. Both may only marry a virgin, may not marry a widow, and may not even incur corpse *tumah* for a close relative; ordinary Kohanim are required not to contract corpse *tumah* such as by attending a funeral with the exception of close relatives. Nor may the High Priests grow their hair long or rend their garments, as normal mourners would, over the death of relatives. Their own deaths serve to enable unintentional murderers who have been banished to one of a handful of the cities of refuge to return home safely, a topic handled in detail in another tractate.

Much food for thought and discussion here. The Gemara starts with a look at how Moses made the anointing oil. A *baraita* explains that he "made it in the wilderness" by boiling spice roots in olive oil. This is R. Yehudah's view of things, and R. Yose quickly interjects that this can not have been the procedure, because given the amount of oil and spices brought with the children of Israel into the desert, it would have all been absorbed into the roots. Instead, he opines, they first soaked the roots in water; they next removed them from the water, and then poured oil on them, thus enabling the oil to absorb the fragrance of the spices. Moses then returned the oil to the appropriate flask. R. Yehudah is not about to take this rebuttal sitting down. He argues that there were plenty of miracles surrounding the oil; the amount Moses brought out of Egypt was used for many things in the Mishkan (Tabernacle), and it was (*Exodus*

30:31) to be "an oil of sacred anointment for your generations" (Alter: "Oil for sacred anointing this shall be…for your generations"), which he takes to be a long, long time—well beyond the literal amount of time it would take to use up the amount Moses carried with him.

Lest one think R. Yehudah's response here was grasping at straws, appealing to miracles by way of explanation, the Gemara introduces another *baraita*. It cites the passage in *Leviticus* (8:10) concerning all the items in the Mishkan (as well as the Mishkan itself) that Moses anointed with his oil. R. Yehudah then sighs at what an extraordinary set of miracles it must have been given the relatively small amount of oil Moses brought with him. In fact, he gets so carried away articulating each and every thing anointed that he mentions kings as well, but the Torah (*Exodus* 30:33) prescribes excision for using the anointing oil on non-Kohanim. The Gemara asks about several kings who were anointed and offers explanations in each case. Bottom line for R. Yehudah is that the oil was to be used for far more things and for an indefinite period of time into the future.

The Gemara proceeds to take apart each of the several cases mentioned a moment ago of kings and priests requiring anointment and looking for scriptural support for each. This *baraita* noted that when a new sovereign accedes to the throne, if he is starting a new royal line and not inheriting it, then he must be anointed. However, another *baraita* then appears to argue the exact opposite, that one king who inherited the throne in the Davidic line required anointing. The Gemara answers this conundrum by explaining that kings in the Davidic line were actually anointed, whereas the kings of the kingdom of Israel were not. In this instance at hand, the king so anointed, Yehu, was from the kingdom of Israel, but because of a succession squabble and his accession to the throne, it was as if he was the first of his family in line. What source, incidentally, supports the argument that privileges those in the Davidic dynasty with anointing oil? Rava cites a verse from *I Samuel* (16:12) calling for anointing of one such king and by implication not others from different lines. But, wouldn't using anointing oil to anoint a non-Davidic king be tantamount to transgression of *meilah*, or inappropriate use of Temple property? Rav Pappa demonstrates that, just as Yehoachaz was anointed with "pure balsam" oil, not with Moses' special oil, so too was Yehu.

When Yehoachaz was mentioned in the *baraita* as being anointed as king, it states the reason being that he was two years junior to his brother Yehoyakim, and anointment was for this reason of jumping over the older son. The Gemara now questions if the difference in ages was what the *baraita* claimed. It turns out that *I Chronicles* (3:15) lists the sons of Yoshiahu and interprets their names in such a way that makes Yehoachaz the firstborn son and Yehoyakim second in line. No, the Gemara responds, in fact Yehoachaz was indeed the "first son" (*bechor*), but only in the sense that he was first to become king, not in age. Oldest sons are supposed to take over the reins of government, as scripture ordains, but the Gemara again parries this potential issue by noting that Yehoyakim was not sufficiently estimable to rule. So, he was passed over.

When listing the sons in *I Chronicles* (3:15), R. Yochanan offered an account of who each of the sons actually was, and the Gemara now wants some better evidence for such an explanation. In the list, a fourth son of Yoshiahu is named as Shallum, whom R. Yochanan claims was the same as Tzidkiyah (also known as Tzidkiyahu), who is listed third—thus, the third and fourth names are actually the same person. A *baraita* is cited that offers the exegetical explanation that "Shallum" acquired his name because of his perfect behavior—"Shallum" meaning complete, cognate with *shalom*. Others, though, claims that his name was a result of the Davidic dynasty ending (coming to "completion") in his time. The Gemara in this string ends with some more permutations on this name.

HORAYOT 12

On the previous *daf* the "anointing" of Yehoachaz when he acceded to the throne was to be understood by the fact that he preceded his brother, but there are still problems with such an explanation. First, there is the question of accessibility of the anointing oil. A *baraita* introduces a scenario in which the Ark was hidden—and with it an assortment of items including the anointing oil—at the bidding of King Yoshiahu, their father. He took this measure to preclude the Babylonians from seizing all of these precious items. Thus, the Levites hid the Ark inside a secret room in the Temple. How we know the other objects—a jar of manna, Aaron's staff, and the flask of anointing oil—were also hidden away is established by R. Elazar through a series of *gezerot shavot*. So, when Yehoachaz came to the throne, the oil was gone, and, as Rav Pappa noted earlier, Yehoachaz was anointed with pure balsam and not Moses' original oil.

We move next to see how the anointing oil was applied. It was apparently smeared over the king's head with a finger to form a crown of sorts. For priests, the oil was smeared "like a *chi*," which Rav Menashya bar Gadda explains is a reference to a Greek letter in the shape of a *kaf*: כ. Scholars in other tractates use the same term but explain it differently, and the rabbis ever since have been unable to come to a consensus about this. This is not to say that they haven't had well-defined positions, just that there is no uniform agreement.

So, then, how did the anointing take place? A *baraita* explains that oil would be poured on the priest's head (pouring) and then it would be smeared on his eyelids (anointing); a conflicting *baraita* explains the procedure in reverse order, first the eyelids and then the head. The first *baraita* in which pouring precedes anointing follows the order prescribed in *Leviticus* 8:12 where Moses poured oil on Aaron's head and then anointed him. The second *baraita* bases its argument on the fact that service items in Temple use are anointed with oil—with no pouring involved—which speaks to the primacy of anointing. Nonetheless, the scriptural verse did effectively stipulate an order: pour and then anoint. The Gemara offers a less than rock-solid rejoinder here: the only reason the oil can be poured is that the anointing has already taken place.

In relation to Moses' anointing of his brother Aaron, the Gemara cites a passage from *Psalms* (133:2) describing the oil spilling onto Aaron's beard and clothing, and two drops were said to have clung to the end of his beard. Rav Pappa claims that, when Aaron spoke with others and apparently waved his beard and head around, those two droplets rose to the roots of his beard where they were safer. Meanwhile, Moses feared that he may have touched those two drops and inadvertently rubbed their residue on himself (self-anointment of sorts) or in some way poured too much oil on his brother (leading to the excess two drops), in either event being cause for fear of committing *meilah*. A *bat kol* (heavenly voice) came to the rescue from on high by announcing, in effect, that this was no case of *meilah*. Moses may have been off the hook, but now Aaron feared that he may have been guilty of committing *meilah*; he may have caused some of the oil to flow to parts of his head or body where it wasn't supposed to go. Wouldn't you know it? Just then another *bat kol*, like the first one citing verses from *Psalms*, proclaimed that Aaron, like Moses, was off the hook.

Where did the actual act of anointment take place? A *baraita* explains that kings would be anointed near a spring as a continually flowing symbol of their everlasting monarchy. A verse from *I Kings* (1:33) offers evidence to this effect.

Anointing a king at a spring is seen to be a "good omen" for the future of the monarchy, and thus the Gemara in the thinnest of segues moves on to a discussion of other good omens. We start with R. Ammi who suggests that, if someone wants to know if he'll live through the end of the year, he should light a lamp between Rosh Hashanah and Yom Kippur in a draft-free home; if the light remains lit until the oil in the lamp burns up, then the answer is yes. If someone is planning a business enterprise and wants to know if success is in the cards, so to speak, he should rear a rooster and if it gets nice and fat, that's a good omen for his future success in business. If someone is planning a road trip and wants to ascertain if he'll return safe and sound, he should stand in a dark house and if he detects a double shadow (lit., "the shadow of his shadow"), that is a good omen as well. All of this smacks of trust in the irrational. To be sure, if (for example) the rooster didn't become fat, that is no foreboding of doom, nor is the invisibility of a second shadow a sign of danger looming along the roads. In fact, the Gemara goes on to caution against the dark house business, because one might be anguished by the inability to make out a second shadow and that might be cause for declining luck. Lest anyone think all of this borderline divination (strictly banned in *Leviticus* 19:26), the rabbis have over the last centuries interpretively precluded such a suggestion.

Abaye adds his two cents now to the topic of good omens by suggesting that one should see and hopefully consume every Rosh Hashanah a gourd, fenugreek, leeks, beets, and dates. There are a number of explanations for these foods, some botanical and others based on language games.

Still recounting stories of omens, Rav Mesharshiyya had occasion to tell one of his sons that he should first study his Mishnah well and then come before his teacher; when sitting in front of his teacher, he should look at the latter's mouth and concentrate on what he is saying. Torah should be studied by a river; as its water surges by without end, so too will the student's knowledge increase. He should also live near the garbage dumps of Mata Mechasya, not near the palaces of Pumbedita; the former implies poorer straits in a city of moral uprightness and few scholars, while the latter is full of Torah scholars but the overall moral air leaves something to be desired. Finally Rav Mesharshiyya advises his son that eating *gildana* (some sort of small fish) about to rot (and hence cheap) is better than consuming *kutach* (a dip or preserve made of sour milk, moldy bread crumbs, and salt) which is expensive and injurious to one's health in the long run.

Edging back from this lengthy digression, the Gemara exegetically explains why the anointing of David and Solomon with oil from a horn led to lengthy reigns in both cases, while the anointing of Saul and Yehu with a flask of oil spelled abbreviated reigns.

Back now fully to our Mishnah and to analysis of the bull offered by the Anointed Priest. In answer to the Mishnah's question as to the identity of this Anointed Priest who offers a bull for mistaken rulings, the text says it's the High Priest. Well, *Leviticus* 4:3 speaks of the "anointed" (*mashiach*), and this term could actually apply to three persons. It might be referring to an anointed king of the Davidic dynasty, but this can't be because the text here adds "kohen." Had the text only included "kohen" but no "anointed," it might have been referring to the High Priest with additional vestments. If the Bible had referred only to "anointed" and not "the anointed," there is a slim chance that it might have meant that a priest anointed for battle—one who would address the troops prior to sending them into battle—was similarly obligated to bring a bull. Thus, the Torah explicitly speaks of "the Anointed Priest," who is superior in station to an anointed priest for battle. How we know this hierarchy is demonstrated, as it were, by an otherwise completely unrelated verse to show that the definite article ("the") is key.

The Mishnah made a point of stating that the bull is the only difference between an anointed High Priest and an (unanointed) High Priest with additional vestments. The latter thus does not bring a bull. But, R. Meir seems to disagree; a *baraita* cites his belief that the latter does bring a bull, a view conflicting with that of the sages. How did R. Meir come to this conclusion? He uses an exegetical tactic which forces the discussion into a long analysis of the Mishnah at hand. The Mishnah has thus far been understood as mirroring the view of the rabbis, not R. Meir.

[a→b]

The Mishnah also only differentiated an attending High Priest from one who substitutes for the attending High Priest (when he must step aside for some reason) by the Yom Kippur bull and the daily one-tenth *efah* of flour. This passage is said to mirror R. Meir's view. R. Meir argued that, after the attending High Priest is compelled to step aside and allow a substitute to fill his shoes, when he returns to office and the substitute steps aside, the latter retains all of the obligations of the anointed High Priest. R. Yose disagrees and argues that the substitute High Priest, once he steps back down, is unfit to serve again either as the High Priest or as an ordinary priest in the Temple. Why not as High Priest? Because he might incur the first High Priest's jealousy. Why not as an ordinary priest? Because—and here is an extremely interesting and recurrent theme in the Talmud—"in sacred matters we elevate but we do not lower" (*ma'alin bakodesh ve'ein moridin*). What this means is that, once a High Priest, the substitute can never return to the lower station of an ordinary priest.

If the way the Gemara has construed authorship of these two sections of the Mishnah is correct, then we have a problem because of different authors. Maybe the first part mirrors the view of the rabbis and the second that of R. Meir. Rav Chisda likes this answer, and this combination is then acceptable. Rav Yosef has another solution: R. Yehudah ha-Nasi assembled the Mishnah, and he selected viewpoints from different, often divergent authorities. Or, a third resolution, the whole Mishnah mirrors the views of R. Shimon who agrees with R. Meir in one instance and disagrees with him in another. A *baraita* is marshaled to support this view. It repeats all those restrictions and duties that distinguish a High Priest from an ordinary kohen. These were outlined on the previous *daf*, but with a few additions here: we learned earlier that a High Priest does not rend his garment in mourning, but here we learn that he doesn't do it from above (the ordinary way) but from below; the High Priest continues to offer sacrifices while an *onen* (someone in the first stage of mourning a close relative, lasting from the death until the end of that day), though he may not consume any of the sacrifices during this period; the High Priest has the privilege of offering his sacrifice first and selecting from any kohanic sacrifice first; he wears the eight vestments while serving in the Temple; he must perform the Yom Kippur services or they are unacceptable; and he is not liable for an offering for any inadvertent act polluting the Temple or its holies.

The *baraita* goes on to note that all of the restrictions and duties mentioned here (and the ones from yesterday) also distinguish the anointed High Priest from the High Priest of additional vestments except the bull; they distinguish the anointed High Priest from the substitute High Priest (who has stepped down) except for the Yom Kippur bull and the one-tenth *efah* of flour; and they distinguish the High Priest (see *Leviticus* 21:10-15) from an anointed priest for battle except for letting his hair grow long, not rending his garment in mourning, not polluting himself for close relatives, the necessity of marrying a virgin, and the ban on marrying a widow. He also enables unintentional murderers to return home. This last point is R. Yehudah's addition, and the sages dispute it.

How does the Gemara know that this *baraita* reflects R. Shimon's thinking? Rav Pappa asks rhetorically: Who exempted a High Priest from an offering due to the inadvertent polluting of the Temple or its holies? His answer is R. Shimon (of course), and we are to assume that this proves the entire *baraita* to be the brainchild of R. Shimon, though this could use a bit more substantiation.

Let's look more closely at the five items noted above that distinguish the High Priest from the priest anointed for battle. For a source here, the Gemara turns to yet another *baraita* which lines up citations from *Leviticus* 21:10-12 with each of these five and offers explanatory interpretation. It uses various hermeneutical techniques of Torah exegesis to do this, and we conclude that the priest anointed for battle is charged with following these same five *mitzvot*. As the Gemara's discussion of this Mishnah comes to a close, one or two incidental cases are raised. Rava asks Rav Nachman if a High Priest who comes down with *tzara'at* must not marry a widow; that is, once he has become High Priest, is he forever forbidden from marrying a widow, or once the affliction has forced him to step down is he now eligible for nuptials with a previously married woman? Unfortunately, Rav Nachman doesn't have a ready answer. But, Rav Pappa asked the same question to Huna son of Rav Nachman, and the latter replied, with an exegesis on a Biblical word considered redundant, that indeed he is permanently so forbidden. Rav Pappa appears to have been very pleased by Huna's answer. The Gemara records that he stood up from his seat, kissed Huna on the head, and proceeded to give his own daughter to Huna in marriage. That's quite an answer—and quite a response to it.

A new Mishnah digresses to clear up one small point raised earlier. We have just learned that a High Priest may rend his garment, upon the death of a close relative, from below, while an ordinary kohen tears it from above. We are, of course, referring to their own clothing; nobody was allowed to rip up priestly vestments (strictly forbidden by the Torah). The High Priest is allowed to make sacrifices while still an *onen*, but he may not eat any part of a sacrifice ordinarily available to a High Priest for consumption. An ordinary kohen neither brings sacrifices nor consumes them while an *onen*.

The Gemara begins by asking about what is meant by below and above. Rav explains "below" literally as the bottom hemline of his garment; same for "above," which means the neckline of the garment. We have not yet met a Rav-Shmuel debate in this tractate, though familiar elsewhere in the Talmud, but Shmuel steps in here and interprets "below" differently; he claims it means just "below" the border, or neckline—the High Priest would poke a hole there and tear from that point up. Shmuel then takes "above" to mean "above" the border. Both renderings thus occur at the neckline in his view.

The Gemara is quick to confront Shmuel's reading here. A *baraita* notes an effective method for rending one's garment which happens to coincide with the way Shmuel describes how the High Priest tears from below—namely, no different from an ordinary rending. Shmuel makes the point that a proper rending must include tearing the neckline; otherwise, it is meaningless. According to the Gemara, Shmuel is in agreement here with R. Yehudah, but it then questions this assertion on the basis of a *baraita* that seems to state that R. Yehudah would not require the High Priest to rend his garments at all. R. Yishmael claims that a High Priest rends no garments in the way that ordinary folk do, but he does do so from below. If R. Yehudah sees no requirement for garment rending on the part of the High Priest, he can't very well be in agreement with Shmuel. The Gemara replies that Shmuel agrees with R. Yehudah that ripping beneath the neckline is meaningless, but he disagrees with him (and agrees with R. Yishmael) that a High Priest should rend (meaningless though it may be) below the neckline.

One more Mishnah on this *daf* examines two sacrificial offerings. If two *mitzvah* duties crop up simultaneously, the one more frequently encountered is given priority. Similarly, anything or anyone of greater sanctity has priority over its counterpart. Thus, if the Anointed Priest's bull and the community's bull are waiting to be offered at the same time, the former precedes the latter.

The Gemara begins by looking for a source for the first phrase of the Mishnah. Abaye cites *Numbers* 28:23 to establish the point, as we have seen any number of times, based on a putative redundancy in the scriptural source. For the second phrase of the Mishnah's opening about the precedence of greater sanctity, the Gemara cites a source (*Leviticus* 21:8) stating that a kohen always goes first: he is called up first to read from the Torah, first to recite the blessing over food, and first to take his portion of food. This is an indication that greater sanctity has its privileges.

HORAYOT 13

This new *daf* begins with the latter part of the last Mishnah we have been looking at, a situation in which both the anointed High Priest and a communal bull are ready to be sacrificed at the same time, and the former goes first by virtue of its higher degree of sanctity. The Gemara, though, wants a source. The verse concerning the communal bull (*Leviticus* 4:21) describes the process "as he burned the first bull." The "first bull" is a reference to the Anointed Priest's bull, thus establishing the order. The Gemara now includes a second source for this Mishnah, this one from a *baraita* that argues logically (on the basis of *Leviticus* 16:17) that the sacrifice of the Anointed Priest's bull affords atonement for the community at large; thus, it only makes sense that the High Priest assumes priority over the community.

This *baraita* goes on to examine the relative primacy of other offerings. Thus, the communal-error bull goes to the Altar before a bull for communal idolatry. Why? The former is a *chatat* (sin offering), while the latter is an *olah* (burnt offering). It takes another *baraita* to explain that one offers a *chatat* first (following *Leviticus* 5:8). Perhaps this verse is only meant to convey a specific case here, but the *baraita* overrides such a presumption and claims that the *chatat*-before-*olah* order is established here as a general rule when the two come to the Altar at the same time.

The first of these *baraitot* mentions another priority ranking, a communal bull for idolatry before a communal male goat for idolatry, both animals being required when a community inadvertently transgresses the laws concerning idol worship. This seems strange, because the former is an *olah* and the latter a *chatat*, indicating the opposite order from what we have just elucidated. The explanation here enters what many uninitiated into the "reasoning" styles of the Gemara may find shaky or worse. A teaching from the Land of Israel is cited: Because the biblical text (*Numbers* 15:24) which discusses the communal-error *chatat* spells this word without an *aleph*, the "deficient" *chatat* (ordinarily spelled with that *aleph*) finds itself deprived of precedence vis-à-vis the associated *olah*. Thus, it is an exception to the rule. Rava suggests that this is due to the fact that in the biblical text the *olah* is mentioned before the *chatat*, thus indicating the exceptional ordering of sacrifices.

From the same *baraita*, another priority ranking: The communal male goat for idolatry comes before the male goat of the Nasi (brought for any inadvertent transgression). Why? Both are *chatat* offerings, but the former is on behalf of the community, while the latter is for a single individual (even if he is the ruler). Also, the male goat of a Nasi comes before the female goat of an ordinary individual (for inadvertent transgressions). Here, the ruler's status trumps an individual ordinary commoner.

Another ruling from our *baraita*: a female goat of an ordinary individual comes before a sheep brought by another ordinary commoner. Here the Gemara responds that another *baraita* taught exactly the opposite order. Abaye explains the rationales behind the (unnamed) authorities of both *baraitot*, without offering a resolution. Finally, the communal meal offering (*omer*) brought on the second day of Pesach comes before the accompanying sheep, an *olah*; and the two loaves of bread brought to the Temple on the festival of Shavuot come before the accompanying sheep offering. For these last two rulings, the general rule is that something brought because of the holiness of a given holiday takes priority over an item brought due to its bread offering. We'll have to see how general this rule is, as it seems to cover only these last two rulings.

While we're on the subject of priorities, a new Mishnah looks at how precedence plays out in environments not involving offerings on the Temple Altar. In matters of saving a life and returning an item that was lost, men take priority over women; in matters involving clothing or liberating from imprisonment, women take priority over men. If both men and women are simultaneously subject to humiliation or molestation, men take priority. Some pretty heady stuff here.

It's one thing when animals and loaves of bread are involved, quite another when human lives are at stake. Let's see what the Gemara can teach us about these rather stark rulings of the Mishnah. According to a *baraita*, if a man is being held against his will together with his father and his teacher, he may be liberated first and his teacher before his father. If his mother is there as well, she takes priority over them all. Furthermore, a sage of the Torah interestingly comes before a king of Israel; the reasoning being that the sage is irreplaceable, while the king always has a successor. A king takes priority over a High Priest; and a High Priest takes priority over a prophet. Both of these dicta are consequences of scriptural verses.

Furthermore, an anointed High Priest takes priority over for the High Priest of additional vestments; the latter takes priority over a High Priest who stepped down because of a polluting seminal discharge; the latter here takes priority over a High Priest who stepped down because he developed a blemish (the *tumah* caused by seminal discharge can be cleared up by a visit to the *mikveh* and waiting for sunset, whereas a blemish can take much more time before it heals completely); a High Priest who stepped down due to a blemish takes priority over a High Priest anointed for battle (the former is expected someday to return to the High Priesthood, while the latter is always an ordinary kohen); the High Priest anointed for battle takes priority over the Deputy High Priest; and the Deputy High Priest takes priority over an *amarkal* (or *amarkol*). What's that, asks the Gemara. Rav Chisda explains that it is a combination of two words, *amar* (he said) and *kol* (everything); it thus refers to the official charged with supervising all Temple functionaries. The *baraita* fills out the list: the *amarkal* takes priority over a *gizbar* (the official in charge of the Temple treasury), a *gizbar* over the chief of a watch, the chief of a watch over a family head, and a family head over an ordinary kohen.

After this extensive inventory of precedence, the Gemara focuses on a single case. When the necessity arises to bury an unattended corpse, one or more persons must perforce contract *tumah*. If only the Deputy High Priest and the High Priest anointed for battle are on hand to perform this *mitzvah*, who does it? The problem is that, because both men are kohens, they are both forbidden from contact with a corpse who is not a close relative. Mar Zutra son of Rav Nachman offers an answer from a *baraita* which states that the High Priest anointed for battle takes on this duty and becomes *tamei*. His reasoning is that, if the Deputy High Priest were to become *tamei* and, for some reason, the attending High Priest should develop a problem on or just before Yom Kippur, the Deputy would be unable to assume the position as his substitute. But, the Gemara notes, the *baraita* just quoted states clearly that the High Priest anointed for battle takes priority over the Deputy High Priest. Ravina offers a compromise solution for the two *baraitot*: this ruling concerning the relative priority of the High Priest anointed for battle was needed because his exhortations to the assembled armies are crucial to the people's very lives; when we are thinking about Temple service, though, the Deputy High Priest comes first.

A new Mishnah, the last one in tractate *Horayot*, continues with the issue of priorities, this time concerning genealogy. Here is the rank order of priority: Kohen > Levi > Yisrael > *mamzer* (child of an illicit match or one whose parent or parents is a *mamzer*) > *natin* (Gibeonites who converted to Judaism at the time of Joshua's conquest, but only to avoid conquest, and Joshua nonetheless honored his pact not to destroy them though consigning them to being water carriers and woodcutters) > convert > liberated Canaanite slave. An important condition: This rank listing only takes effect when the persons involved are of equal intelligence. Example: a *mamzer* who is a Torah scholar takes priority over a High Priest who is an idiot, one of my favorite aphorisms of the entire Talmud. It theoretically affords a way out of having to deal incessantly with an ignoramus in the highest of ritual posts. We have all faced similar situations in life. How might such a fool become a High Priest? Good question, asked apparently by many of our scholars over the years, though one without any easy solution. Perhaps not complete idiots, there were any number of High Priests in the Second Temple period whose behavior left much to be desired.

Let's start unpacking that first string of priorities by citing sources to support them. For the first two—Kohen > Levi, and Levi > Yisrael—the Gemara cites two appropriate biblical verses. For the next one—Yisrael > *mamzer*—the Gemara argues "logically" that a *mamzer* lacks the genealogical purity of a Yisrael. And, a *mamzer* > *natin* because at least the *mamzer*'s father has Jewish ancestors, whereas the father of a *natin* descended from Gibeonites. Perhaps most puzzling, at least as a modern reader is the penultimate link in the chain—*natin* > convert—which is justified by the fact that the *natin* was raised in a Jewish realm, while the convert presumably was not. The liberated slave sits at the very bottom of the totem pole, because he was once execrated. The Gemara then asks how we know the final condition—that this ordering takes effect when the persons involved are of equal intelligence. The answer comes from R. Acha bar R. Chanina who quotes *Proverbs* 3:15 and interprets it to mean that the Torah is more cherished than even a High Priest at the Temple. When all is said and done, though, custom has dictated that, when available, virtually any Kohen will be called to the Torah first, even if a brilliant *mamzer* is a member of a given congregation. (This situation, *mutatis mutandis*, still prevails.)

The Gemara now goes back to a section of the Mishnah and cites a germane *baraita*. R. Shimon bar Yochai suggests that, by rights, because a liberated slave would have grown up among Jews, he should have priority over a convert, but the law rules the other way around because of the former slave's debased past. Hardly seems fair. Some students are recorded next asking their teacher, R. Elazar son of R. Tzadok, why some Jewish men want to marry a convert but not a liberated slave (despite the fact that her status is higher than that of a convert). He gives the same answer—her execrable past, which the female convert happily lacks (at least, lacks having been a slave). Also, the convert may have been contemplating conversion and thus may have kept chaste while still a gentile, behavior apparently alien to a former slave.

This exchange leads to two more, though unrelated to the matter at hand. Why does a dog acknowledge its master, but a cat does not? R. Elazar son of R. Chanina answers: We know that anyone who consumes something which a mouse has gnawed at acquires a tendency to forget; if he or it consumes a mouse, as do cats, out goes memory altogether. How is it that mice are at the utter bottom of the entire animal kingdom, controlled by all others? Answer: They are evil creatures by nature, through and through. How so, asks the Gemara. Rava helps by explaining that mice not only nibble away at food but also at clothing, from which they gain nothing but cause harm to humans.

[a→b]

Rav Pappa offers a similar response.

Having totally digressed, the Gemara decides to live it up a bit and moves into a fascinating discussion of causes of forgetfulness. A *baraita* cites five things that cause one to forget one's acquired wisdom: (1) eating something that a mouse or cat has already gnawed at; (2) eating the heart of an animal; (3) eating olives on a regular basis; (4) drinking leftover bathwater; and (5) washing one's feet with one atop the other. Others add to the list putting one's clothing beneath one's head for a pillow. By stark contrast, there are also five things taught in this *baraita* which help revive one's wisdom: (1) eating bread from charcoal (interpreted by one authority as meaning well-baked bread); (2) eating soft-boiled eggs with no salt; (3) consuming olive oil on a regular basis; (4) consuming wine and fragrant spices on a regular basis; and (5) drinking water after it was used to make dough. Others add to this list sticking one's finger in salt and eating it (the salt).

The third item of reviving lost wisdom, consuming olive oil, jibes well with a teaching of R. Yochanan who juxtaposed it with the third item concerning forgetfulness. Eating lots of olives may cause loss of accumulated knowledge, but olive oil helps restore it. Similarly, the fourth item on the revival list is reflected in Rava's (seemingly immodest) reflection that his own consumption of wine and aromatic spices made him wise. What about the final item of reviving knowledge? Resh Lakish insists that the digit sticking must be done with a single finger. A *baraita* records R. Yehudah supporting the single-finger thesis, but R. Yose insists on two and not three fingers. The Gemara even offers a mnemonic—*kemitzah*—to help remember this dispute. When making a flour offering, as described in great detail in tractate *Menachot* (Meal offerings), one folds his fourth or ring finger down to hold a modicum of flour in the palm. When doing so, it leaves the pinky by itself on one side and two fingers (the thumb doesn't count here) on the other—one and two. Why one needs a mnemonic for something this simple is not explained.

Having broached the topic of things that aid and hinder learning, the Gemara now unfolds a list of ten things injurious to the learning process, many (if not all) of them, it must be averred, pure superstition: (1) walking under a camel's halter; (2) walking between two camels; (3) passing between two women; (4) a woman passing between two men; (5) walking near to something giving off the malodorous stench of a carcass; (6) walking beneath a bridge under which no water had flowed for forty days; (7) consuming bread not fully baked; (8) eating meat with the spoon used to stir the grease on the pot's surface; (9) drinking water from a brook running through a cemetery; and (10) staring into a corpse's face. Others add to the list: reading the writing on a gravestone.

Rather than comment on this list, the Gemara makes an abrupt segue to a discussion about ways of according Torah sages proper honor. When the head of the Sanhedrin (called the Nasi here) comes into the study hall, everyone there rises in respect, and they sit down only when he instructs them to do so. When the second in command, the *av bet din* (head of the court), comes in, the scholars there rise and make a row on either side of him, while others present may remain seated. When a sage comes in, the scholars within a four-cubit radius rise when he approaches, and they sit when he passes out of their orbit. Sons and students of sages, when needed, are permitted to traipse among and through everyone assembled in the study hall. Numerous further details about leaving and coming are now added to this mix: who can sit in front of whom, facing whom, backs to whom, and the like. One such is that a scholar who needs to urinate is allowed to do so and then return to his seat; one could hardly expect otherwise. But, Rav Pappa claims that this only holds for urinating; defecation is unacceptable, for one who has the need should have done so first thing in the morning or should wait until evening. Why? Because he shouldn't be away from his fellows for too long a period of time, and everyone knows elimination can be time-consuming.

R. Yochanan offers a bit of the background to this long *baraita* and its injunctions about proper honors. It dates back to the era when Rabban Shimon ben Gamliel was head of the Sanhedrin; R. Meir was the greatest sage of the time; and R. Natan was *av bet din* (head of the rabbinical court). When any one of them came into the study hall, all those present rose out of respect. Rabban Shimon ben Gamliel felt there should be a distinction in the honors accorded him and that accorded the others. He thus proclaimed the *baraita* we have been examining. The next day when R. Meir and R. Natan entered the study hall, they did not receive the same greeting from the assembled scholars. They were outraged until informed of Rabban Shimon ben Gamliel's decree. So they decided to somehow counter this measure. They planned to call him in and ask him to explain the extremely difficult Mishnaic tractate *Uktzin* (Stalks), which they believed he had not as yet learned well; then, they would use this to knock him down a peg and remove him from his high post. Can such plans come to fruition? Well, most certainly not. R. Yaakov ben Karshi heard them plotting and was dumbstruck, horrified at the humiliation it would cause Rabban Shimon ben Gamliel. So, he dug out tractate *Uktzin*, and began studying it out loud and repeatedly within earshot of Rabban Shimon ben Gamliel who realized that something nefarious was up and it involved *Utzkin*. So he devoted himself to mastering this tractate. Sure enough, the very next day, R. Meir and R. Natan invited him to teach them about tractate *Uktzin*, and that is precisely what Rabban Shimon ben Gamliel proceeded to do. He finished with them by noting that, had he not studied the tractate the previous day, it wouldn't have been so fresh in his mind, and they would have brought humiliation upon him. Thereupon, the two conniving rabbis were booted out of the study hall.

And, there they stayed, communicating with the other scholars inside by writing questions on stone tablets and tossing them inside and back outside. Ultimately, R. Yose realized that this was an unsatisfactory means of exchanging views—someone could get hurt—and that R. Meir and R. Natan were important minds, and he went with his colleagues to ask Rabban Shimon ben Gamliel to rescind his expulsion order. He relented but with the proviso that thereafter no Torah ruling from them would be identified in their own names. R. Meir would henceforth be referred to as *acherim* (others), and R. Natan as *yesh omrim* (some say). Later still, heaven visited a dream on the two rabbis that they should attempt to appease Rabban Shimon ben Gamliel further. R. Natan did so, but not R. Meir because he thought dreams were inconsequential and bore no special meaning. R. Natan's efforts earned him the rebuke of Rabban Shimon ben Gamliel.

Our tractate *Horayot* concludes on the next *daf*.

HORAYOT 14

At the tail end of the previous *daf*, the Gemara was about to offer an example of the punishment visited on R. Meir. When R. Yehudah ha-Nasi, redactor of the Mishnah, was teaching his son, Rabban Shimon, a Mishnah found in tractate *Bechorot* (First born), he referred to R. Meir as *acherim* (others). The son asked his father about the identity of these unnamed "others" (which he understood full well) and implied that "they" were important scholars. R. Yehudah ha-Nasi replied that "they" are those who tried to dishonor our household. Father and son then each marshaled a biblical citation, the son suggesting that their deeds were long over and done, the father suggesting that the impact of their deeds remained. Rabban Shimon isn't denying that R. Meir and R. Natan were guilty, only that their actions were ultimately ineffective. They had failed. R. Yehudah ha-Nasi, interestingly, then goes back to the Mishnaic text he had been teaching his son and replaces "others" with "in the name of R. Meir." Rava points out that he didn't go all the way to stating "R. Meir said," but attributed the Mishnaic teaching to him indirectly. So, the son teaches the father a modicum of consideration.

In an abrupt segue, the Gemara now has R. Yochanan introduce a difference of opinions between Rabban Shimon ben Gamliel and the rabbis, though we don't know which side held which opinion.

One side claims that a "Sinai"—a man whose intellectual distinction can be found in his breadth of learning in Mishnayot and *baraitot*, and on their basis whose rulings are as crystal clear as the day they were given at Sinai—is more desirable that a man who "uproots mountains" (because of his incisive powers of analysis and exegesis). The other side reverses these preferences. Rav Yosef was a "Sinai" and Rabbah was an "uprooter of mountains." A group of rabbinic students was looking for someone to head their academy and asked which of the two sorts would be a better fit for them. They were told that a "Sinai" was more desirable, and so asked Rav Yosef to lead them. Rav Yosef, though, declined, and Rabbah accepted in his stead. And, Rabbah went on to serve in that capacity for twenty-two years. This piece of homiletic learning ends with a somewhat cryptic note that Rav Yosef during that entire time never even let a bloodletter into his home, presumably meaning that he never accepted anything that even remotely smacked of leadership, perhaps (and only perhaps) because he did not want even a whiff of possible humiliation to blow from him in Rabbah's direction—I was asked first but turned it down, and that's why you got the job—and thus the point of this story is counterpoint to the earlier tale about R. Meir and Rabban Shimon ben Gamliel.

The Gemara ends with another story. This one finds four scholars—Abaye, Rava, R. Zera, and Rabbah bar Matnah—agreeing that they needed a leader. They decide that the first of them to offer a teaching that is not contested will be the leader. But, as one may easily imagine, all of their opinions are contested by one another—all, that is, except Abaye. Thereupon, Abaye was invited by Rava to present a Talmudic address. As our tractate comes to a close, we find R. Zera and Rabbah bar Matnah, the other two scholars who were part of this story, being compared. The former was more on the "uprooter" side of the spectrum, while the latter pursued analysis through to the very end. Which one is more desirable? *Teku*, the matter remains unresolved, as it remains until this day.

And so ends tractate *Horayot*. Decisions, decisions, decisions. There seems to be no end to cases requiring them—not then and not now.

Glossary of Selected Terms

Amora (pl. Amoraim): scholars from Babylonia and the Land of Israel who commented on and discussed the law, ca. 200–500 C.E., and whose debates constitute the bulk of the Gemara

Annointed Priest (Kohen mashiach): usually the High Priest, descendants of Aaron

asham: guilt offering

asham talui: suspended (variable) guilt offering

baraita (pl. *baraitot*): oral laws not codified in the Mishnah and with slightly less authority

chatat (pl. *chataot*): sin offering brought to the Temple for sacrifice; divided into inner and outer *chataot*

daf (pl. *dapim*): a Talmudic folio page

eglah arufah: calf decapitated as part of the ritual following the discovery of a corpse whose murderer is unknown; see *Deuteronomy* 21:1-9 for details

Gemara: collected commentary, discussions, and debates on the Mishnah

gezerah shavah (pl. *gezerot shavot*): argument by verbal analogy; when a word appears in two, sometimes three, separate places in the Bible, the laws and meanings surrounding one apply to the other as well

High Priest (Kohen gadol): descendants of Aaron, head of the Kohanim

High Priest with additional vestments: reference to the special additional vestments worn by the High Priest

karet: excision; one of the most severe punishments for a transgression

kemitzah: extraction of the flour offering using the middle fingers of the right hand

kezayit: olive's volume, minimal amount of food whose consumption legally constitutes eating

kiddushin: betrothal

kilayim: forbidden mixtures, such as wool-linen garments

mamzer: offspring of an adulterous or incestuous coupling, or child of a *mamzer*.

meilah: illicit use of Temple or Tabernacle property

Mishnah (Mishnayot): collection in six "orders" and numerous tractates of the laws of the Torah; also, the individual rulings in each tractate

Nasi (pl. *Nesiim*): prince, head of the Great Sanhedrin; head of one of the twelve tribes

natin: a descendant of the Gibeonites who agreed to peace, under false pretenses, with Joshua at the time of the conquest of Canaan; Joshua kept his side of the bargain nonetheless but assigned them the perennial status of woodchoppers and water-carriers

nesech wine: wine associated with pagan libations

nevelah (pl. *nevelot*): animal that died by means other than ritual slaughter

niddah: a woman post-menstruation but prior to submersion in a *mikveh* which concludes purification

olah (pl. *olot*): burnt offering

onen: the initial stage of mourning a close relative; lasts from the death until the end of that day *par helem davar shel tzibur*: communal-error bull

R.: rabbi

Resh Galuta: descendant of the Davidic dynasty, leader of Babylonian Jewry

rosh yeshivah (most eminent member of the court)

Sanhedrin: assembly of 20-23 judges of most communities; Great Sanhedrin of 71 judges served as a Supreme Court

tamei: ritually impure (adjective describing *tumah*; see *tumah* below)

Tanna (pl. Tannaim): commentators of the Mishnah, ca. 70–200 C.E.

Tanna Kamma: anonymous first voice of a Mishnah or *baraita*

teku: let it stand unresolved (rabbinic decision)

temurah: exchanged animal to be sacrificed

terefah (pl. *terefot*): animals with one of a number of specified physical problems

teyuvta: rabbinic refutation

tumah: ritual impurity

tzara'at: skin affliction often mistranslated as leprosy

Index of Tannaim and Amoraim

(Note: Names are as cited in the text—JAF.)

Abaye, 4–5, 7, 8, 32, 38, 39, 40, 41, 42, 44, 47, 79, 84, 86, 95
Ben Azzai (Shimon ben Azzai), 8, 18, 21
Chizkiyah, 22, 58
Huna son of Rav Nachman, 83
Mar Zutra son of Rav Nachman, 88
R. Abba, 5
R. Acha bar R. Chanina, 89
R. Acha bar Yaakov, 34, 39
R. Akiva, 18, 21, 55, 56, 58
R. Ammi, 78
R. Chiyya, 73
R. Elazar, 18, 20, 38, 77
R. Elazar son of R. Chanina, 90
R. Elazar son of R. Tzadok, 17, 90
R. Eliezer, 30, 57, 59
R. Meir, 12–13, 20, 27, 29–30, 31–33, 35, 37–38, 80–81, 92–94
R. Natan, 92–94
R. Shimon, 13, 14, 18, 19–20, 24, 27, 28, 29–30, 31, 31–33, 34, 35, 38–40, 41, 42, 57–58, 62, 69, 70–71, 81, 82
R. Shimon bar Yochai, 90
R. Shimon ben Elazar, 13, 31, 33
R. Shimon ben Yose, 6
R. Yaakov ben Karshi, 92
R. Yehoshua, 17, 64
R. Yehoshua ben Levi, 52
R. Yehudah, 9–10, 11–12, 13, 19, 27, 28, 29, 30–31, 32–33, 34, 35, 38, 71, 74–75, 82, 84, 91
R. Yehudah ha-Nasi, 49–50, 51, 52, 53, 73, 81, 94
R. Yirmyah, 55
R. Yishmael, 25, 84
R. Yochanan, 6, 20, 34, 59, 66, 70, 76, 91, 92, 94
R. Yonatan, 16–17
R. Yose, 74, 81, 91, 93
R. Yose Haglili, 54–55
R. Yose son of R. Yehudah, 72
R. Zera, 20, 24, 70, 95
Rabbah bar Bar Chanah, 65, 72
Rabbah bar Matnah, 95
Rabban Gamliel, 64
Rabban Shimon ben Gamliel, 17, 92–95
Rabban Yochanan ben Zakkai, 64–65
Rami bar Chama, 6
Rav, 6, 67–68, 83
Rav Acha, 40, 72
Rav Ashi, 18, 22, 30, 33
Rav Assi, 13–14
Rav Avdimi bar Chama, 64
Rav Chisda, 26, 65, 81, 87
Rav Dimi, 4–5
Rav Hamnuna, 71
Rav Huna, 18
Rav Huna son of Rav Hoshaya, 16
Rav Huna son of Rav Natan, 59

Rav Huna son of Rav Yehoshua, 58, 65
Rav Kahana, 35
Rav Menashe ben Gadda, 77
Rav Mesharshiyya, 17, 79
Rav Nachman, 12, 82, 88
Rav Nachman bar Yitzchak, 22, 26, 56, 67
Rav Nachman bar Rav Chisda, 65
Rav Pappa, 6, 11, 13, 36–37, 47, 59, 65, 76, 77, 78, 82, 83, 90, 92
Rav Safra, 73
Rav Shaba, 35
Rav Sheshet, 25, 59, 70
Rav Yehudah, 9–10, 11, 19, 67
Rav Yosef, 24, 38–39, 41, 81, 95
Rav Zevid, 69–70
Rava, 5–6, 7–8, 21, 32, 40–41, 47, 56, 58, 65, 67, 69, 76, 83, 86, 90, 91, 94, 95
Rava son of Rabbah, 64
Ravina, 5, 24, 56, 72, 88
Resh Lakish, 66, 91
Shimon ben Zoma, 8
Shmuel, 4, 5, 9, 12, 83–84
Sumchos, 20
Ulla, 22, 55, 67, 70

Index to Biblical and Rabbinic References

Genesis 13:10, 66
Genesis 48:4, 34, 40
Genesis 48:6, 40
Exodus 18:22, 26
Exodus 30:31, 74–75
Exodus 30:33, 75
Exodus 34:14, 24
Leviticus 4:3, 44, 45, 48, 51, 62–63, 80
Leviticus 4:13, 16, 19, 28, 48
Leviticus 4:14, 29, 51
Leviticus 4:13-14, 30
Leviticus 4:18, 51
Leviticus 4:21, 85
Leviticus 4:22, 62, 63
Leviticus 4:22-23, 71
Leviticus 4:22-26, 62
Leviticus 4:27, 9
Leviticus 5:5, 55
Leviticus 5:8, 85
Leviticus 5:18, 50
Leviticus 6:2, 12
Leviticus 6:13, 56
Leviticus 8:10, 75
Leviticus 8:12, 77
Leviticus 16:17, 85
Leviticus 16:33, 39
Leviticus 19:26, 79
Leviticus 21:8, 84–85
Leviticus 21:10-12, 82

Leviticus 21:10-15, 82
Numbers 8:8, 35
Numbers 8:12, 35
Numbers 11:16, 26
Numbers 15:24, 31, 86
Numbers 15:26, 32
Numbers 15:27, 50, 53
Numbers 15:28, 49
Numbers 15:29, 53
Numbers 15:29-31, 52
Numbers 23, 68
Numbers 28:23, 84
Deuteronomy 17:8-11, 22
Deuteronomy 17:15, 55
Deuteronomy 21:8, 37
I Kings 1:33, 78
I Kings 8:65, 13
II Kings 15:5, 64
I Chronicles 3:15, 76
II Chronicles 20:5, 34
I Samuel 16:12, 76
Ezra 3:13, 37
Ezra 8:35, 35
Hosea 14:10, 65
Kohelet 8:14, 65
Proverbs 3:15, 89
Proverbs 18:1, 67
Proverbs 18:19, 67
Psalms 45:17, 36

Psalms 133:2, 78

Bechorot, 94
Keretot 19a, 30

Menachot, 91
Sanhedrin 86b, 4–5
Uktzin, 93
Yevamot 87b, 5

www.ingramcontent.com/pod-product-compliance
Lightning Source LLC
Chambersburg PA
CBHW070645300426
44111CB00013B/2264